THE RIGHT *to* WRITE

THE RIGHT *to* WRITE

AN INVITATION AND INITIATION INTO THE WRITING LIFE

JULIA CAMERON

JEREMY P. TARCHER/PUTNAM

a member of Penguin Putnam Inc.

NEW YORK

In order to preserve my friends' and students' privacy,
certain names have been changed.

Most Tarcher/Putnam books are available at special quantity discounts
for bulk purchases for sales promotions, premiums, fund-raising, and
educational needs. Special books or book excerpts also can be created
to fit specific needs. For details, write Putnam Special Markets,
375 Hudson Street, New York, NY 10014.

Jeremy P. Tarcher/Putnam
a member of
Penguin Putnam Inc.
375 Hudson Street
New York, NY 10014
www.penguinputnam.com
First Trade Paperback Edition 1999

The Library of Congress has cataloged the hardback edition as follows:

Cameron, Julia.
The right to write: an invitation and initiation into the writing life /
Julia Cameron.
p.   cm.
ISBN 0-87477-937-5
1. Authorship.   I. Title.
PN151.C275   1998   98-22242 CIP
808'.02—dc21
ISBN 1-58542-009-3 (paperback edition)

Printed in the United States of America
15 17 19 20 18 16 14

This book is printed on acid-free paper. ∞

Book design by JUDITH STAGNITTO ABBATE

Acknowledgments

I AM INDEBTED TO

Mark Bryan

The Camerons

Sonia Choquette

Michelle Esrick

Rhonda Flemming

Roland Flint

Joel Fotinos

Natalie Goldberg

Sister Julia Clare Greene, BVM

Erin Greenberg

David Groff

Gerard Hackett

Arthur Kretchmer

Laura Leddy

Emma Lively

Larry Lonergan

Ellen Longo

Michele Lowrance

Julianna McCarthy

William McPherson

James Navè

John Newland

John Nichols

Will Nix

David Saltz

Susan Schulman

Domenica Cameron Scorsese

Max Showalter

Roger Slakey

Martha Hamilton Snyder

Johanna Tani

Jeremy Tarcher

Martin Torgoff

Edmund Towle

Dori Vinella

Tim Wheater

Aura Wright

FOR MY WRITING MOTHER,
DOROTHY SHEA CAMERON

Contents

INTRODUCTION

In December 1967, under the baleful gaze of a gargoyle high in an upper cranny of Georgetown Library, I came across a line from the poet Theodore Roethke. He wrote, "I learn by going where I have to go." That phrase accurately describes my writing life.

I've written since I was very young and, as I get older, I write more and more frequently, in more and more genres. I have written fiction and nonfiction, films, plays, poems, essays, criticism, journalism, and even musicals. I have written for love, for money, for escape, for grounding, to tune out, to tune in, and to do almost anything that writing could be made to do.

Writing has for thirty-plus years been my constant companion, my lover, my friend, my job, my passion, and what I do with myself and the world I live in. Writing is how, and it sometimes seems why, I do my life.

My story is simple: I simply write. I have tried, in this book, to write only about the things I know, only about the things that have been my tools, my path. This means that there are many things that will not be included in this book because they are either not a part of my writer's experience or they are something other books on writing have written about very well.

This book will not teach you how to write a query letter, how to find a market for your work or get an agent. It will not teach you to punctuate or spell. Anton Chekhov advised actors, "If you want to work on your acting, work on yourself." This same advice applies to working on our writing.

Our writing life, our life "as a writer," cannot be separated from our life as a whole. For this reason, many of the essays and especially the "tools" in this book "about writing" may, at first flush, seem to have nothing to do with writing—but they have everything to do with writing. Think of each essay as an invitation to explore a certain area. Think of each tool as an experiential initiation into that area.

What this book will do, if I have done it well enough, is talk to you about writing for the sake of writing, for the sheer unadulterated joy of putting words to the page. In other words, this is less a "how-to" book than a "why" book.

Why should we write?

We should write because it is human nature to write. Writing claims our world. It makes it directly and specifically our own. We should write because humans are spiritual beings and writing is a powerful form of prayer and meditation, connecting us both to our own insights and to a higher and deeper level of inner guidance as well.

We should write because writing brings clarity and passion to the act of living. Writing is sensual, experiential, grounding. We should write because writing is good for the soul. We should write because writing yields us a body of work, a felt path through the world we live in.

We should write, above all, because we are writers whether we call ourselves writers or not. The Right to Write is a birthright, a spiritual dowry that gives us the keys to the kingdom. Higher forces speak to us through writing. Call them inspiration, the Muses, Angels, God, Hunches, Intuition, Guidance, or simply a good story— whatever you call them, they connect us to something larger than ourselves that allows us to live with greater vigor and optimism.

It is my hope that this book will dismantle some of the negative mythology that surrounds the writing life in our culture. I have found that life to be positive, invigorating, spiritually sourced, and eminently do-able. This book, therefore, will be an "into the water" book as we look at common blocks and some simple ways around them, common problems and some simple ways to solve them, common sticking points and some simple ways through them. In my experience, the writing life is a simple life, self-empowered and self-empowering.

This book will be a cheerleader for those trying the writing life, a companion for those living it, and a thank-you to my own writing for the life it has given to me. It is my hope that this book will help to heal writers who are broken, initiate writers who are afraid, and entice writers who are standing at river's edge, wanting to put a toe in.

I have a fantasy. It's the pearly gates. St. Peter has out his questionnaire, he asks me the Big Question, "What did you do that we should let you in?"

"I convinced people they should write," I tell him. The great gates swing open.

BEGIN

I AM SITTING AT a small pine table, facing east toward the Sangre de Cristo foothills. My "view" has a horse tank that needs filling, a white fence with a small robin's-egg-blue gate, a birdbath in terra-cotta with some of its figurines knocked off, a bright yellow garden hose I will use to fill the horse tank and the birdbath, an overgrown garden plot, a bucket lying on its side, my small dog, Maxwell, soaking in the early spring sunlight like an optimistic sunbather on a chilly beach day. When it warms up and that yellow hose has thawed out, I will fill the horse tank. When I warm up, I will tell you what I know about letting yourself write.

The first trick, the one I am practicing now, is to just start where you are. It's a luxury to be in the mood to write. It's a blessing but it's not a necessity. Writing is like breathing, it's possible to learn to do it well, but the point is to do it no matter what.

Writing is like breathing. I believe that. I believe we all come into life as writers. We are born with a gift for language and it comes to us within months as we begin to name our world. We all have a sense of ownership, a sense of satisfaction as we name the objects that we find. Words give us power.

As toddlers, first we grab and then we grab with words. Every word we learn is an acquisition, a bit of gold that makes us richer. We catch a new word and say it over and over, turning it like a rich nugget in the light. As children, we hoard and gloat over words. Words give ownership: we name our world and we claim it.

As children, we learn new words at an astonishing clip. Words give us leverage: "Me go with Mommy!" Or, "Mommy stay." Children are specific and direct. They don't beat around the bush. Their words are personal and powerful. They are filled with will and intent. They are filled with passion and purpose. Children trust the power of words.

If words give us power, when do we start to lose our power over words? When do we start to feel that some of us are "good" at language and even have a shot at being "writers" while the rest of us just happen to use it and don't dare consider ourselves in that league?

My guess is that for most of us school is where this sorting starts to happen. School is where we are told, "You're good with words . . ." The neat teacherly scrawl, diagonally written across the top right-hand corner of the top page of, say, a geography report on Scandinavia, "Well written."

Well written—what does that mean? In school it usually means clear, orderly thinking. Neat enough grammar. Lots of orderly facts. It may also mean things we are taught, like "topic sentences" and "transitions." Very often it does not mean words that sing off the page, innovative word combinations, paragraphs of great free associations and digressions—all the gifts a young poet or novelist might have and want to use but not find useful under the scholarly discipline of an academic paper.

What happens when writing of that kind shows up in school papers? Too frequently, it's another margin quote, this time negative: "You stray from the topic a bit here" or "Stick to the point." It is a rare teacher who takes the time and care to praise the kind of writing that doesn't fit into an academic paradigm. It's as though scholastically we're on a pretty strict diet: "Not so much pepper here."

Not so much pepper. Not so much spunk. Not so much humanity, please. Academically we are inclined to a rather pedestrian prose denuded of personality and passion, perhaps even a bit elevated in tone as if writing is something to be done only from the loftiest of motives, a kind of distillate of rationalism trickled onto the page.

In countries and situations where writing is forbidden, it takes on primacy. In prisons, people scratch their message into stone, onto dirt. On desert islands, messages are shoved into bottles and set to sea. When communication is made to seem actively impossible, the human will to communicate rears its head and people willingly risk death and dismemberment to do it.

This is healthy.

In our current culture, something much less healthy is afoot. Writing is not forbidden, it is discouraged. Hallmark does it for us. We shop for the card that is "closest" to what we wish to say. Schools drill us about how to say what we want to and the how-to involves things like proper spelling, topic sentences, and the avoidance of detours so that logic becomes the field marshal and emotion is kept at bay. Writing, as we are taught to do it, becomes an antihuman activity. We are forever editing, leaving out the details that might not be pertinent. We are trained to self-doubt, to self-scrutiny in the place of self-expression.

As a result, most of us try to write too carefully. We try to do it "right." We try to sound smart. We try, period. Writing goes much better when we don't work at it so much. When we give ourselves permission to just hang out on the page. For me, writing is like a good pair of pajamas—comfortable. In our culture, writing is more often costumed up in a military outfit. We want our sentences to march in neat little rows, like well-behaved boarding-school children.

Burn down the school. Save the books, perhaps, but get the teacher to tell you the real secrets: What does he write and read as a guilty pleasure? Guilty pleasure is what writing is all about. It is about attractions, words you can't resist using to describe things too interesting to pass up. And forget lofty motives.

I don't write from lofty motives—I never have. In sixth grade, when I wrote my first (very) short stories, it was to snag the attention of Peter Mundy—Peter was a newcomer to St. Joseph's grade school, Mrs. Klopsch's class. He'd moved north from Missouri. He brought a southern accent and chestnut hair, hair the color of a jar of Tupelo honey, a physical look as sweet as the something southern that whispered through his voice. I wanted Peter to be my boyfriend. I wanted him to notice me. And so, I set about wooing him by writing him stories.

Twenty years later, long after he'd dated Peggy Conroy instead of me, Peter told me I had captured his heart with my writing, "I just chickened out."

Peter may have chickened out, but in the act of chasing him with pencil and paper, I discovered a bigger chase, the thrill of chasing anything with words.

Writing is a lot like driving a country blacktop highway on a hot summer day. There is a wavery magical spot that shimmers on the horizon. You aim toward it. You speed to get there, and when you do, the "there" vanishes. You look up to see it again, shimmering in the distance. You write toward that. I suppose some people might call this unrequited love or dissatisfaction. I think it's something better.

I think it's anticipation. I think it's savoring. I think it's tasting a great meal from its scent on your nostrils. I do not have to eat freshly baked bread to love it. The scent is nearly as delicious, nearly as much the satisfaction as the thick slice of bread slathered with butter and homemade apricot jam.

The brain enjoys writing. It enjoys the act of naming things, the processes of association and discernment. Picking words is like picking apples: this one looks delicious.

The act of writing, the aiming at getting it right, is pure thrill, pure process, as exciting as drawing back a bow. Hitting a creative bull's-eye, a sentence that precisely expresses what you see shimmering on the horizon—those sentences are worth the chase—but the chase itself, the things you catch out of the corner of your eye, that's worth something too. I love it when I write well, but I love it when I write, period.

When I began this essay, it was a blue, cloudless day. As I finish it, big weather has come up. Fat, dark clouds are spitting a petulant rain. The wind is gusting in stiff puffs fragrant with spring. I don't need to fill the horse tank. The rain is doing that nicely. My little Maxwell has come inside and is cuddled by my feet. The day, like this essay, began one place and moved to something else entirely.

Kabir tells us, "Wherever you are is the entry point," and this is always true with writing. Wherever you are is always the right place. There is never a need to fix anything, to hitch up the bootstraps of the soul and start at some higher place. Start right where you are.

Left to its own devices, writing is like weather. It has a drama, a form, a force to it that shapes the day. Just as a good rain clears the air, a good writing day clears the psyche. There is something very right about simply letting yourself write. And the way to do that is to begin, to begin where you are.

BEGIN
Initiation Tool

This tool puts you directly into the water. Take three sheets of 8½ by 11 paper. Start at the top of page one and for three pages describe how and what you are feeling right now. Begin where you are—physically, emotionally, and psychologically. Write about anything and everything that crosses your mind.

This is a free-form exercise. You cannot do it wrong. Be petty, critical, whining, scared. Be excited, adventurous, worried, happy. Be whatever and however you are at this moment. Get current. Feel the current of your own thoughts and emotions. Keep your hand moving and simply hang out on the page. When you have finished writing three pages, stop.

LET YOURSELF WRITE

WE PUT A LOT of bunk around the notion of being a writer. We make a big deal out of putting words on paper instead of simply releasing them to the air. We have a mythology that tells us that writing is a torturous activity. Believing that, we don't even try it or, if we do, and if we find it unexpectedly easy, we stop, freeze up, and tell ourselves that whatever it is that we're doing, it can't be "real" writing.

By real writing we mean the kind we have all the mythology about. We mean the kind that does not involve scenarios like the one I had tonight: a dinner with my good friend Dori, watching *Il Postino* on video afterward, kissing Dori good-bye when it was still mid-evening, and strolling into my study to write just a little while little dog Maxwell curls at my feet.

There is something too casual, too effortless, too normal about this kind of writer's life. It too closely resembles everyone else's life—just with some writing sandwiched in. Why, if this is how a writer lives, lots of us could do it. If the suffering is actually optional, if writing needn't be an antisocial activity . . .

What if there were no such thing as a writer? What if everyone simply wrote? What if there were no "being a real writer" to aspire to? What if writing were simply about the act of writing?

If we didn't have to worry about being published and being

judged, how many more of us might write a novel just for the joy of making one? Why should we think of writing a novel as something we couldn't try—the way an amateur carpenter might build a simple bookcase or even a picnic table? What if we didn't have to be good at writing? What if we got to do it for sheer fun?

What if writing were approached like white-water rafting? Something to try just for the fact of having tried it, for the spills and chills of having gone through the rapids of the creative process. What if we allowed ourselves to be amateurs (from the Latin verb *amare,* "to love"). If we could just get over the auditioning to be respected at this aspect, a great many people might love writing. Although our mythology seldom tells us this, it's fun.

When people undertake writing, it is often not with the agenda of writing but with the agenda of "becoming a writer." We have an incredible amount of mystery, mystique, and pure bunk around exactly what the phrase means.

The bottom line, the fact that the act of writing makes you a writer, barely enters the equation at all. Instead, we come up with ideas like "Real writers are published," or "Real writers make a living from their writing." In a sense, we are saying, "Real writers get validation from others that they are writers. Their passport is stamped in ways that indicate they are writers. They have appeared in _____. They have received quotes from _____."

With mythology like this, with a product-not-process orientation like this, is it any wonder that the aspiring writer is seized by anxiety? Even those gifted with a silver tongue doubt that they are gifted with a silver pen. The blank page strikes them like a blank check where they may be asked to fill in an amount far larger than the talent they feel they possess.

"I'd love to be a writer. I just have no gift for it," I've often been told by people whose gift of language is as clear as a neon sign.

"I'm a good talker, but I can't write to save my life" is another thing I've been told quite often. Where do we get the idea that putting words on paper is so dangerous and so difficult?

There is something that often happens as people try to move onto the page: the fluidity they feel in talking suddenly freezes up. Every word becomes a commitment, a matter for intense scrutiny and self-absorption. The blank page creates a sense of seriousness. Words that sounded fine suddenly look funny. We forget the term "rough draft" and want everything to emerge as well-polished gems. There's no place for error, for colloquialisms, for the charming roundabouts. Our schooling kicks in and we remember all those rules for good writing: topic sentences, organization. . . .

Most of us think we can't write. We think it's something other people do—"writers." Or, if you have a novice's happy skill and amateur's fervent love, it's a name you reserve for the skill belonging to "real writers." The kind of people who can march their thoughts like little soldiers, marshal their logical paragraphs like troops storming Normandy, a scintillating wave at a time.

It doesn't have to be like that.

If we eliminate the word "writer," if we just go back to writing as an act of listening and naming what we hear, some of the rules disappear. There is an organic shape, a form-coming-into-form that is inherent in the thing we are observing, listening to, and trying to put on the page. It has rules of its own that it will reveal to us if we listen with attention. Shape does not need to be imposed. Shape is part of what we are listening to. When we just let ourselves write, we get it "right."

LET YOURSELF WRITE
Initiation Tool

This tool clears away the debris that stands between you and the page. Set aside one half hour. Go to a café with writing paper. Buy yourself a cup of coffee, tea, a soda, or mineral water. Write out the following exercise.

Step one: What are your hidden associations with the term "writer"? Fill in the following as rapidly as possible.

1. Writers are _____
2. Writers are _____
3. Writers are _____
4. Writers are _____

5. Writers are ————————————————
6. Writers are ————————————————
7. Writers are ————————————————
8. Writers are ————————————————
9. Writers are ————————————————
10. Writers are ————————————————

Step two: Convert the negative associations to positive affirmations. For example: "Writers are broke" converts to "Writers are solvent." "Writers are crazy" converts to "Writers are sane." "Writers are loners" converts to "Writers have good friends." For the next week, write out each of your new positives five times daily.

LET YOURSELF LISTEN

O NE OF THE simplest and smartest things I ever learned about writing is the importance of a sense of direction. Writing is about getting something down, not about thinking something up. Whenever I strive to "think something up," writing becomes something I must stretch to achieve. It becomes loftier than I am, perhaps even something so lofty, it is beyond my grasp. When I am trying to think something up, I am straining. When, on the other hand, I am focused about just getting something down, I have a sense of attention but not a sense of strain.

Another way to think of it is that writing is the art of taking dictation, not giving it. When I listen to what I hear and simply jot that down, the flow of ideas is not mine to generate but to transcribe. When, on the other hand, I struggle to write, it is because I am trying to speak on the page rather than listen there.

Once writing becomes an act of listening instead of an act of speech, a great deal of the ego goes out of it. Instead of self-consciously thinking about the sentence "I" have written, I find myself amazed and interested by the sentences that seem to want themselves written. Instead of being an act of pontification, writing becomes an act of revelation. This is true for any writer who lets writing write through him. We the writers, as much as any reader, are in for the treat of discovering what comes next.

When writing is about the importance of what we ourselves have to say, it becomes burdened by our concerns about whether the reader will "get it"—meaning, get how brilliant we are. When writing is rooted in the process of taking down the next thought as it unfolds itself to us, then it is less about our brilliance and more about our accuracy. How carefully are we willing to listen? How much control are we willing to surrender for the sake of allowing creativity to move through us rather than our trying to flog it forward for agendas of our own?

We can either "think a plot up" or we can "jot a plot down." We can either "think of something to write about" or we can write about what we happen to be thinking about. We can either demand that we write well or we can settle more comfortably into writing down what seems to want to come through us—good, bad, or indifferent.

Most of us are really willing only to write well, and this is why the act of writing strains us. We are asking it to do two jobs at once: to communicate to people and to simultaneously impress them. Is it any wonder that our prose buckles under the strain of doing this double task?

Of all the writers writing on writing I have ever read, it seems to me that Henry Miller was the most honest, the least self-serving and self-mythologizing. Miller advised:

"Develop interest in life as you see it; in people, things, literature, music—the world is so rich, simply throbbing with rich treasures, beautiful souls, and interesting people. Forget yourself."

When we "forget ourselves," it is easy to write. We are not standing there, stiff as a soldier, our entire ego shimmied into every capital "I." When we forget ourselves, when we let go of being good and settle into just being a writer, we begin to have the experience of writing through us. We retire as the self-conscious author and become something else—the vehicle for self-expression. When we are just the vehicle, the storyteller and not the point of the story, we often write very well—we certainly write more easily.

LET YOURSELF LISTEN
Initiation Tool

This tool encourages you to lighten up and stop taking writing so seriously that it is frightening. Pretend that you are sitting under a large tree with your back resting on its trunk. On the other side of the tree, a Storyteller sits also resting against the tree trunk. Take a sheet of paper and number from one to five. Tell the Storyteller five things you'd like to hear stories about.

The Time Lie

If I had a year off, I'd write a novel."

Maybe you would. Maybe you wouldn't. Often the greased slide to writer's block is a huge batch of time earmarked: "Now write." Making writing a big deal tends to make writing difficult. Keeping writing casual tends to keep it possible. Nowhere is this more true than around the issue of time.

One of the biggest myths around writing is that in order to do it we must have great swathes of uninterrupted time. Speaking for myself, I have never had such silken bolts of time. My life—and all the work I have made from my life—has been more like making a patchwork quilt than unfolding bolts of limitless and serene silk.

The myth that we must have "time"—more time—in order to create is a myth that keeps us from using the time we do have. If we are forever yearning for "more," we are forever discounting what is offered.

Just at the moment I have out-of-town guests coming in, a meal to cook, horses to feed, and my dogs would really like a good long walk. I may or may not get to the "long" part of walk, but I will get to everything else—right after I write. Years as a single mother, a full-time teacher, and a full-time fiction writer taught me to grab for time to write instead of wait for time. Grabbing is what I am doing right now. Grabbing works.

For most of us, the seductive and unstated part of "if I had enough time" is the unstated sentence "to hear myself think." In other words, we imagine that if we had time we would quiet our more shallow selves and listen to a deeper flow of inspiration. Again, this is a myth that lets us off the hook—if I wait for enough time to listen, I don't have to listen now, I don't have to take responsibility for being available to what is trying to bubble up today.

As a teacher, I have often heard, "All that stands between me and the great American novel is a year off." Viewed this way, the obsession with a block of time becomes writer's block. Most students—most of us, period—are not going to be given the gift of a year off. And without that year off, we can't "really" write, can we?

Maybe we can.

The "if-I-had-time" lie is a convenient way to ignore the fact that novels require being written and that writing happens a sentence at a time. Sentences can happen in a moment. Enough stolen moments, enough stolen sentences, and a novel is born—without the luxury of time.

Lawyer Scott Turow wrote his riveting novel *Presumed Innocent* on his daily commuter train. My student Maureen has managed nine full-length screenplays while raising an infant son and juggling a design career. Michael, another student, wrote an entire book in his "spare" moments the year that he got his master's degree. All of them did it by making time to write rather than waiting to "find" time.

When we make time to write, we can do it anytime, anywhere. Once we learn the knack of "dropping down the well"—a knack I teach by having people write three pages of longhand first thing in the morning—the well can be dropped down anywhere, anytime: in your dentist's office, on an airplane, at the train station waiting for someone else's commuter train, between appointments at the office, at lunch, on a coffee break, at the hairdresser's, at the kitchen table while the onions sauté . . .

If we learn to write from the sheer love of writing, there is always enough time, but time must be stolen like a quick kiss between lovers on the run. As a shrewd woman once told me, "The busiest and most important man can always find time for you if he's in love with you and, if he can't, then he is not in love." When we love our writing, we find time for it.

The trick to finding writing time, then, is to write from love and not with an eye to product. Don't try to write something perfect; just write. Don't try to write the whole megillah; just start the whole megillah. Yes, it is daunting to think of finding time to write an entire novel, but it is not so daunting to think of finding time to write a paragraph, even a sentence. And paragraphs, made of sentences, are what novels are really made of.

Annie, a newspaper writer by trade, was always waiting to "find" the time to write for pleasure. This made it sound like time was a hundred-dollar bill that she might stumble on in the street one very lucky day.

"Don't wait to find time," I told her. "Get aggressive. Steal time."

Annie found she could steal fifteen minutes a day at first. Then she found she could manage it twice a day. Before too long she was managing stolen hours, twice a week. Like an unexpected love affair, Annie's pleasure in writing caught her by surprise, insinuating itself gently into her heart. She suddenly "had" time.

Alan, a writing teacher and a yearning-to-be-novelist, told himself for years that his novel would come once he took a sabbatical. One day he made the mistake of telling the same thing to me.

"What's wrong with now?" I asked him. "Start writing now and think about rewriting on the sabbatical."

"I don't have time," Alan protested. "I teach writing. I sit there and watch my students write." He sounded bitter and grumpy.

"So write while they're writing. Stop making it such a major production. Just scribble a few things while they do."

"I get these ideas but I don't know exactly where they're going," Alan protested.

"So chase one and see where it leads."

"Chase one! What if it's a dead end? I don't have time for dead end!"

"There are no dead ends, not really," I assured him. Alan was cornered, and he knew it.

Alan had time to write. We all have time to write. We have time to write the minute we are willing to write badly, to chase a dead end, to scribble a few words, to write for the hell of it instead of for the perfect and polished result.

The obsession with time is really an obsession with perfection. We want enough time to write perfectly. We want to write with a net under ourselves, a net that says we are not foolish spending our time doing something that might not pay off.

"Start with Morning Pages," I urged Alan. "Let yourself get on the page. Write three pages about absolutely anything. It will train your censor to let you create."

"I'm dubious," Alan told me.

"Be dubious. But try," I nudged.

Dubious didn't matter. Morning Pages successfully primed the pump. Before a few weeks had passed, Alan was racing his students to the page. A sentence at a time, a page at a time, he was writing. He was even chasing what would have once struck him as a dead end.

"I think I am a better teacher too," he tells me.

I am not surprised. Nothing communicates more clearly than love, and Alan's love of writing lit him like a lamp for his students to see by.

When we let ourselves write from love, when we let ourselves steal minutes as gifts to ourselves, our lives become sweeter, our temperaments become sweeter. We are no longer envious bystanders standing on the sidelines and muttering, "I'd love to, but . . ."

"If I lived in Key West, then I could find time to write. . . ."

"If I had more in savings, then I could find time to write. . . ."

The lies we tell ourselves about writing and time are all connected to envy, to the fairy tale notion that there are others whose lives are simpler, better funded, more conducive to writing than our own.

The trick to finding writing time is to make writing time in the life you've already got. That's where you've got leverage. Stop imagining some other life as a "real" writer's life. Key West sunsets do not make a writer's life. Trust funds do not fund the flow of ideas. All lives are writers' lives because all of us are writers.

Laura teaches gifted kindergarten students. Her days are busy with lesson plans, papers to grade, parents to confer with. In the midst of all this, Laura makes time for three pages of morning writing and some afternoon writing sandwiched in before dinner. Some weeks she adds writing time on Saturdays. For the past two winters she has also taken writing classes at a nearby community college.

"I used to moan that I never had any time to write," Laura remembers. "I wanted to write and I resented not writing but I also felt safe. It was threatening to begin to make time for writing, but making the time has changed everything. I now not only have time to write, but I seem to have time to do other things as well. Frankly, I think I was depressed and writing got rid of my depression. Is that possible?"

"Writing 'rights' things," I told Laura.

"I know you've always said that, but I never believed it," she answered. "Now I do."

Taking the time to write in our lives gives us the time of our lives. As we describe our environments, we begin to savor them. Even the most rushed and pell-mell life begins to take on the patina of being cherished.

THE TIME LIE
Initiation Tool

We often say, "I don't have time to write." But we do have time to write—a little. This tool helps you to start dismantling your sense of victimization around time. Buy five postcards and five stamps. Locate the addresses of five people you love but don't take time to stay in touch with. Set the clock for fifteen minutes. Using two to three minutes per card, write out loving greetings to your friends. Stamp the cards and mail them.

TRACK

THERE SHOULD BE some artier way of saying it: I think of it as laying track. If you are America and you let yourself lay track, writing will let you move coast to coast, mapping your interior, enjoying the sights.

I believe that what we want to write wants to be written. I believe that as I have an impulse to create, the something I want to create has an impulse to want to be born. My job, then, is to show up on the page and let that something move through me. In a sense, what wants to be written is none of my business.

Early in my writing life, I tried to polish as I went. Each sentence, each paragraph, each page, had to flow from and build on what went before it. I thought a lot about all of this. I really worked at it. I toiled at being a writer. This meant long, stubborn hours writing and rewriting, crossing out and then adding back in again. Writing this way was frustrating, difficult, and disheartening, like trying to write a movie and cut it at the same time.

The danger of writing and rewriting at the same time was that it was tied in to my mood. In an expansive mood, whatever I wrote was great. In a constricted mood, nothing was good. This made writing a roller coaster of judgment and indictment: guilty or innocent, good or bad, off with its head or allowed to go scot-free. I wanted a saner, less extreme way to write than this. I wanted emotional sobriety in my writing.

Aiming for that, I learned to write setting judgment aside and save a polish for later. I called this new, freer writing "laying track." For the first time I gave myself emotional permission to do rough drafts and for those rough drafts to be, well, rough.

Freed to be rough, my writing actually became smoother. Freed from the demand that it be instantly brilliant, perfect, and clever, my writing became not only smoother but also easier and more clear. When I went back to polish, I found there wasn't that much to fix or change. A remarkable amount of my first-draft material withstood the test of later scrutiny.

I had never realized that all of my drama around writing was exactly that, drama. I had never realized that drama about the page had little to do with the real drama that was supposed to exist on the page.

Dismantling the drama, like dismantling a loaded gun, filled me with a sense of relief. I stopped being superstitious. I didn't need to circle my desk eighteen times like a dog looking for a place to lie down. Wherever I began was where I began. I remembered that once upon a time, writing had been fun for me. My job was to do the writing, not judge the writing. I discovered that the writing seemed to contain an inner plan of its own. For me, writing is like listening to a melody line in my head. Note by note it knows where it wants to go. I follow it and lay it down. I can pare it, shape it, polish it later. For the moment, my job is just to get it down, just to catch the thought, which I can add to or embellish later on.

Over the years I have learned that there is a pattern or form being formed like a crystal in the subconscious of an artist. Growing in darkness by dribs and drabs, over time it makes a magnificent formation. My job is to take down the dribs and the drabs—to free-associate, if you will, knowing that the associations have their own plans for where we're going with all this.

Composer Eric Satie remarked that he liked to "walk around a piece a few times" before writing it. I walk around an idea, taking notes as I go. If something comes up and suggests itself, I let it have its say. I am curious about where every apparent detour is really leading. I have learned to let the patterns reveal themselves instead of demanding that they have a logical flow at the time. I have learned that as far as writing goes, my logic brain is for second drafts. My rich, fertile, whimsical brain is for laying track.

I do not worry about going up blind alleys. Most alleys lead somewhere, and if it's just to a box where I corner myself into saying something I didn't expect, that's all right too. I know there are people who polish as they go along. That's not how I do it. Instead, and maybe this is some American throwback to the stories of building the great railways, I think of it as laying a trail from point A to point B. Every day, for at least a few minutes, I try to lay some of the track. I do not set a goal for how much track I will lay. I used to do that, and when I did, I set the goal low: three pages of screenplay or a page and a half of prose. This was, for me, a workable amount. It meant ninety pages of first-draft screenplay in a month. It meant forty-five pages of first-draft prose. It meant, in short, that I was laying track.

There are people who worry about how to lay out the best trail. To me, that's a little topiary and advanced. The "best" trail is for second drafts. The getting from point to point, the drive across country, is the first draft. First drafts that are allowed to find their own shape and form very often do find the best trail or something very close to it. Writing that is overplanned and overrehearsed is juiceless. Later drafts, then, are about pumping it up. How much better to have a wild and somewhat unruly first draft, something that can be shaped and tamed, something so full of detail, it's a question of what we want to leave in, not a question of what still needs to be added.

When in doubt, put it in: the man with the thrilling voice who leaves messages on your answering machine, the bossy blue jay who is commandeering the bird feeder, the letter you didn't get today for all of your waiting. Put it in. Disguise it if you must, but put it in. Writing is big—big enough to hold everything small you want to put into it. Writing is passionate. Passionate enough to withstand whatever mood you've got, whatever temper is dragging you around by the tail.

Writing—and this is the big secret—wants to be written. Writing loves a writer the way God loves a true devotee. Writing will fill your heart if you let it. It will fill your pages and help to fill your life.

TRACK
Initiation Tool

Writing helps us map our interior world. Part of laying track is letting ourselves imagine what directions we might like to lay it in. This tool helps you get a sense of your emotional geography.

If you didn't have to actually write it, what might it be fun to write? A mystery? Short stories? A novel? Songs? Plays? Poetry? You may be attracted to many different forms of writing—and that is OK. It doesn't mean you're a shallow dilettante. It means you are multifaceted. Take fifteen minutes and write, longhand, as fast as you can, about the kinds of writing it would be *fun* to do.

BAD WRITING

THE SKY TONIGHT is doing high drama. There's a stiff wind, dark, scudding clouds, quick pellets of a rain that stings but doesn't pour. In the west, the sunset is a slender strip of apricot silk lying along the horizon—the silk of a Carole Lombard negligee, ripe, soft, and seductive. The whole evening is like an affair that can't quite get started. Now we've got great bolts of lightning—they drop like cartoon swords, jagged and bright yellow-gold—the kind that the gods used in the animated version of Greek mythology. If I write about this evening long enough, it flirts with the mind: "Go riding before it gets dark—No, it's going to rain." "Stay in and read a book. It's a nice rainy night, but—there's that sunset. Go out and look at that, will you? Are you crazy? The lightning . . ."

Writing doesn't always have to know where it's going. Yes, yes, in school we are taught to march our thoughts in nice orderly rows—as though that's the way they occur to us. As if that's the way we really think. The writing we learn in school—in most schools—is a stripped down, chromeless, noncustomized prose. Unlike this evening, it wouldn't have any fancy lightning bolts and certainly not in combination with a Carole-Lombard–peignoir set of clouds.

Writing like that—"good" writing—is like watching a movie we've seen before. We can admire the craft, but none of the outcome chills us to the marrow, moves us to tears, or causes us to gasp with recognition. Sometimes it takes "bad" writing to do that. Bad writing—when it's good—is like New York street pizza. Sometimes it's a little too crusty. Sometimes it's a little soggy, but the tang is undeniable. It has flavor. Spice. Juice.

And so, in order to be a good writer, I have to be willing to be a bad writer. I have to be willing to let my thoughts and images be as contradictory as the evening firing its fireworks outside my window. In other words, let it all in—every little detail that catches your fancy. You can sort it out later—if it needs any sorting.

I know a beautiful woman who always ruins a good outfit by adding some outlandish something—a veiled hat, a poinsettia for God's sake tucked behind an ear, a giddy chiffon scarf. This is a woman that men adore. Even while her "sisters" sniff at her fashion errors, men trail after her in fascination. There's something a little enchanting about the mix and match that doesn't match. There's something a little wild, a little exotic, about the stray feather stuck inexplicably in her cleavage, the gaudy vintage pin festooning her hat.

Prose can benefit from a little lurid frippery. The understated, carefully modified, exclamation-points-only-with-papal-permission prose that we learn in school that actually bores a lot of us out of writing. "If you can't say anything nice—or nicely—don't say anything at all," we are taught, and we learn the lesson well. If only we could give ourselves permission to write "badly," so many of us would write very well indeed.

I got a phone call from Caroline, a young writer finishing her college degree. Caroline is a feisty writer whose prose snorts with spirit. She is witty, pointed, poignant—but not this time.

"I am writing a paper and it's miserable," she wailed. "Can I read you some of it?"

"All right. A little," I reluctantly agreed. Who wants to hear something "miserable"?

Caroline began reading. Her sentences marched like dutiful soldiers. There was no fire, no passion, nothing but duty, duty, duty running across the line. It was "good" writing at its worst.

"Stop!" I begged. "What happened?"

"You tell me!" Caroline yelped.

"Well, it sounds very, very careful," I said. "Like you're not really saying what you think."

"I'm not!" Caroline confessed. "I'm scared to say what I think. I hate this professor. He's a nitpicker and everything I love he hates and vice versa. I'm trying to write something he will like."

"Maybe you have to choose between being a good writer and being a good student."

"At least I'd respect myself. So, what do you think I should do? Tear it up and start again?"

"Actually? Yes. Throw that out and start over. Say what you mean and mean what you say. You'll like yourself and your writing a lot better."

Caroline headed off to write again.

What is it, I wondered, that makes "good" writing so terrible sounding?

Two hours later Caroline called back.

"Listen to this," she said, her voice strong and merry.

I listened to a paper filled with crisp, crackling prose and prickly opinions. Caroline laughed as she read.

"He may hate it, but this is really what I think," she finished.

"So you've raised the stakes, haven't you?" I asked her. "Now it matters—and because you let yourself care, maybe your professor will be coaxed into caring too."

I got off the phone and thought: "That's it. So much 'good' writing doesn't seem to care."

It's too cool, cerebral, calculated, and calibrated. Therefore: I love to read the tabloids. The tabloids are full of good "bad" writing.

Like the twentieth-century version of a Dickens potboiler, tabloids are compulsive reading. Intricate in high-stakes story lines, they are as rich as high-fat ice cream. The beauties are all "breathtaking." The villains all "hideous." Victims are universally "helpless" and "innocent." Murders are "grisly."

In the tabloids, unlike life, the stakes are always high. Lovers are betrayed. Spouses are duped. Treachery lurks at every turn—as do loyal dogs who rescue drowning men from raging floods.

More people read the tabloids than read *The New York Times.* The tabloids write about ESP, recipes for surefire sex, twins reunited after fifty years. In the tabloids, people see angels, small voices save them from certain death, loyal cats return across continents.

I like to buy my tabloids in clumps of five. I like to read five different versions of the week's headline news. *The Globe. National Enquirer*—who's got it right? It's all in the details. The bloody handprint. The tiny glove. The letter delivered after seven years in the mail. The tabloids love surprises—and so do we. Surprise is what "good" writing has whipped out of us.

Caroline phoned to report that her professor had succumbed after all to her fine and feisty paper. She sounded revved up.

"And guess what?"

"What?"

She'd just written a small, very noir short story "just for the hell of it."

"Writing just for the hell of it is heaven, isn't it?" I asked.

"Yeah," came her hardboiled reply. "Yeah. Maybe it is."

The evening has settled down. Carole Lombard has finally gone to bed. The lightning bolts have stalked off somewhere else. I am sure it was bad writing to talk about all of it. Yes, and it was fun.

BAD WRITING
Initiation Tool

Perfectionism is a primary writer's block. We want to write—we just want to do it perfectly. With this tool you will deliberately indulge in some "bad writing."

Step one: Go to the supermarket or newstand. Buy three tabloids. Perhaps the *National Enquirer, The Star, The Globe.* If you cannot find tabloids, buy *People* or *Us.* Scissors in hand, read your tabloids. Snip out ten stories that strike you. Some of you may choose an ESP story, some a money story, others a story of murder and mayhem. One type of story may attract you more than others. Clip your stories together and save them in a file folder. Did you notice any common denominators in the stories that interested you? Were they upbeat or downbeat? Weird? Kinky or heartwarming?

Step two: Set aside one half hour. Writing as fast as you can, longhand, write a make-believe tabloid story. Make up characters, incidents, and quotes. Be outrageous. Meet and marry aliens from outer space. Discover your long-lost twin. Survive a grizzly attack. Win five million dollars. Write boldly and badly. Scribble this story off. At the end of one half hour, stop writing.

This Writing Life

Outside the study window, the horses are cued up waiting for me to feed them breakfast. They are hungry and cranky—the way I feel when I don't write. For me, writing is an appetite, a joy. Even when I don't think I want it, even when I think I have nothing to say, it seduces me like the first really balmy day of spring: I want out of whatever I am doing and into it.

I have crawled out of lovers' beds to sneak off and write. Pregnant with my daughter, I stayed up late the night before she was born because I had to write about her entry point into the world. I stayed up late, wrote, and when the labor pains—an inaccurate word, the contractions, the tightening of a band of muscles that is as mysterious and involuntary as kundalini energy—when those started, I woke my husband and said, "Now." But not until I had gotten the "now" on paper.

There is a great happiness in letting myself write. I don't always do it well, or need to, but I do need to do it. There is a great and simple satisfaction, like tagging base with a real friend. There is a "me" that emerges in relationship to writing, like the "me" that emerges in certain friendships, who makes me laugh.

I suppose that the psychologically inclined could find grounds for narcissism in a love of writing. Who cares? I believe that we are meant to move through the world with interest, and writing keeps me interested. It is like comparing notes.

I do not experience writing as a monologue. I experience it as a conversation. Writing raises questions "I" hadn't thought of. Writing offers "me" a different perspective, a different and more engaging way to look at things.

Poet James Nave calls this "poetic vision." He claims that all of us have it if we will just give ourselves permission to see the poetry that surrounds us. He talks about focusing a minute at a time, a thing at a time, on whatever catches our interest. This is what the Buddhists call living mindfully. I call it living "heartfully" and buried in that word "heart" is the word "art" and another word, "ear." Writing is the art of a listening heart.

Writing this, I see that I am talking about the same kind of benefits people mention when they talk about their meditation practice. "I see things differently" and "things come to me."

Things do come to us through writing, and they are not always so intangible as insights. Moving our hands across the page, we make a handmade life. We tell the Universe what we like and what we don't like, what is bugging us and what is giving us delight. We tell the Universe and ourselves what we would like more of, what we would like less of, and through this clarity a shift occurs. Writing is a psychological as well as a physical activity. When I "clear my thoughts," I am literally rearranging my life itself.

A woman I know well just went through a season of depression. A lover whom she cherished moved half a continent away. He seemed to take her joy in living with him. She took to her bed.

"I just wanted to stay in bed under the covers for the rest of my life," she told me. "Then I thought, 'I might as well write while I am lying there.' Once I started writing, I started to lighten up. It gave me a way to move through my feelings. I think I quite literally had to digest what happened to me, and writing let me do that."

My friend thinks of writing as digestion. For me, it is that and more. For me, writing is food itself. I need a certain amount of writing to stay healthy. Some people like to write in binges, but I like to write three times a day. I quite literally write the way I eat, with appetite and delight at the things I savor.

agree — important

Sometimes what I savor is an event—or even the anticipation of an event. Other times, it is a phrase, a thought that I get curious about, tasting it in my mouth like a fruit.

Recently I have made a new friendship with a very tall and busy man who lives in Manhattan. Yesterday, it occurred to me, "David has a vertical life." I meant that his days are long and steep with work, that each day is a climb through activities, a surge like a jet climbing to clear sky again at midnight.

My life here in New Mexico, on my ranchito the size of a taco chip, is not vertical. It is horizontal. On three sides I am surrounded by mountains. On the fourth side I look west for a hundred miles over, past and through mountains.

As a writer, I am always staring at distance, always looking at something moving toward me from a long way off, not only weather—the rain stalks across the plain on legs—but also people, events, and situations. I love staring into distance. I love squinting at the image of things yet to come. I love the process of watching them come into focus.

That focusing is writing. It begins as an image, something I want to see more clearly. Writing then becomes like the act of focusing a set of binoculars and setting down what appears. It is description of "the movie in my mind," as writing teacher Colleen Rae calls it. It is observing and writing something down, not thinking something up.

If we let ourselves notice, writing feels collaborative. It is a dance between reality and us as an observer. This is true even in writing fiction. Just like the Sacred Mountain outside my window exists and is real, the whatever it is that we are trying to write already exists and is real. Our job is to respond to that existence, to take it in and take it down. Our job is to pay attention.

My red Arab, Jack, is staring at the study window with focused attention. I know that he can hear the tapping of keys. I know that for him my writing is both the delay before he is fed and the signal that he will soon be fed. He counts on my writing as do I.

"I don't know how you do it," I am sometimes told when I am embarking on some creative pas de deux that looks risky to others—a new book with an old husband, perhaps.

Writing is how I do "it." Writing is how I do everything. Writing is how I metabolize life. It is food for thought and it is food itself. If a difficult situation comes up in my life, I write at it as well as write about it.

Earlier this week I had a vicious and damaging conversation with an editor. A piece of my writing had been heavily and badly rewritten. I called to complain. I called to say, "I am a grown-up. Let me do my own changes, shape my own work." What I got, in saying this, was a sudden and personal attack.

The editor is a writer who is not writing. I am a writer who is writing happily and often. The attack came from misery laced with vitriol and envy. It came like a wasp sting, with drunken swaying, heavy with poison. I got off the phone reeling—stung. Then I thought of that editor, dour and vicious as a medieval gargoyle, and wrote out my own medicine.

MISERY

O misery. It is difficult to walk
With thorns in your feet.
The sting, the bleeding—
Why is it you are not heeding
Your longing for another path?

O misery. You are walking on glass.
Your sole is cut and torn.
Why have you shorn your raven locks,
Why do you stumble dreamless in your pain?

Misery, I remember you before the hemlock.
I remember you proud and fierce.
Before you drank the drink of self-forgetting,
You were glorious, an exquisite gyre,
Turning in the sun.

Misery, what have you done?
Why do you pluck your feathers
Bleeding by your own beak?

Misery, speak to me. Say your name.
Say the shame you feel not saying it.

Misery, remember who you are.
That long and jagged scar:
Own what you've done—
This costly dance with bloody feet on jagged stone.
Own what you've done, forgive it and come home.

Writing is alchemy. Writing that poem, moving out of the cramped and cerebral space of bitterness into the capacious heart, I am no longer a victim, an enemy, an injured party. I am what I am again: a writer. I have metabolized the injury into art.

"I've never seen anything like it," a doctor once told me. "You go straight from injury to art."

Writing is medicine. It is an appropriate antidote to injury. It is an appropriate companion for any difficult change. Because writing is a practice of observation as much as invention, we can become curious as much as frightened in the face of change. Writing about the change, we can help it along, lean into it, cooperate. Writing allows us to rewrite our lives.

My mother once remarked—catastrophically, to my soon-to-be husband, a jealous man—"Julie has a habit of keeping her old boyfriends."

This is true, but it is because my old boyfriends become something else—my old friends. Writing makes that possible. Relationships are like landscapes: they are beautiful, and the light we see them by changes with the seasons. Writing helps this to happen. Writing allows us to give the characters in our life different plot lines. It allows the face of love to change, to be redrawn.

We can use writing the way a filmmaker uses a lens: to pull focus, to put things into a different perspective. We can zoom into a close-up. We can pull way back and put something against a larger swathe of landscape. If writing is observing the movie in our minds, it is also editing it, adding sound track, putting on a voice-over.

I have a girlfriend who says that we all get the God we deserve. What a scary phrase! I've altered it: we all get the God we can relate to. I am an artist and the past thirty years have been spent looping through plots, meeting up with characters. Is it any surprise that my God features highly dramatic turns of events—entrances and exits worthy of the movies? Writing helps me to chart these events, savor their unfolding.

When I met my new friend David, he stepped through a curtain and held out his hand. He stepped through a curtain . . .

Writing that phrase, I have a click of recognition: I had drawn a curtain around my life. I wasn't expecting anybody to show up bold enough not to be deterred. Ah-ha, an interesting turn of events, a turn of events that I noticed because of a turn of phrase.

The turn of phrase is the turn of a key: it unlocks the door, it turns the motor over. A key and a pen both fit the hand, and they both take only the simplest of motions to start things moving, changing, altering . . . I dip my pen into life the way I dip a paddle into a river. I add velocity, change direction, stride and glide. The muscles of my mind, like the muscles of my body, love the splash and jostle of the creative river. It is taking me somewhere, but I am shaping my trip as we go. I can lie back or crunch forward. I can eddy along the shore or head for the swift flow at the center. It is an adventure. I like this writing life.

THIS WRITING LIFE
Initiation Tool

We are often so busy wanting to have a life as a writer that we forget that we have a life to write about. In this tool you will practice the writing about your life.

Light a candle. Cue up a piece of soothing music. Set aside fifteen minutes. Writing longhand, describe a situation in your life that you are currently trying to metabolize. Some examples:

- Getting used to my new boss
- My anger at my sister
- Actually living with my boyfriend
- Worrying about my dog's health
- Whether I should buy a mountain bike

MOOD

I AM NOT IN THE MOOD to write today. My thoughts are cranky and resistant. I feel sluggish, irritable. I do not want to write. My body of information feels like that of an out-of-shape athlete. The only one who has been doing sit-ups is my censor.

No matter that I have been writing now, full-time, for thirty years. Today my censor is saying, "What do you know about writing?" One thing I know about writing is that you do not have to be in the mood to do it.

Being in the mood to write, like being in the mood to make love, is a luxury that isn't necessary in a long-term relationship. Just as the first caress can lead to a change of heart, the first sentence, however tentative and awkward, can lead to a desire to go just a little further. All of us have a sex drive. All of us have a drive to write.

The drive to write is a primary human instinct: the drive to name, order, and in a sense control our experience. The drive to write, that primal glee we felt as children when we learned the letters that formed our name and then the words that formed our world, is a drive that has been buried in our frantic, electrical, telephonic age.

"E-mail" is a rebalancing of the wheel. People love e-mail because they love to write. Furthermore, because it is instantaneous, e-mail tricks people into evading their censor. E-mail isn't "real" writing. It's something more casual and quirky and inventive. It's somehow naughty and anarchistic, like passing notes in school. E-mail tempts us into writing because it's a nonauthoritarian place to write. We can dash off quick notes, break thoughts in the middle, say, "I'll get back to you later." E-mail allows us intimacy without formality. No wonder we love it. It lets us drop the rock.

When we let writing be a Big Deal, it is difficult to do it. When we find that without our wanting it to, writing has become a Big Deal, we need to learn to negotiate. I negotiate by bribes: "Write for twenty minutes and then you can watch that documentary on Henry Miller."

Elizabeth, a writer-editor for a children's press, negotiates by breaking everything down into tiny, do-able steps.

"A lot of the time when I am not in the mood to face a whole project I will say, 'Just turn on the computer and write one paragraph. That's all.'" When she does her one paragraph, Elizabeth usually finds that it leads to two, three, a small chunk of work that gets down because she "tricked" herself with the promise that she had to do only an itty, bitty bit.

"I'm not saying the part of me that writes is dumb, but it can be easily fooled and easily bribed," she laughs. "I tell it 'only ten minutes, sweetie,' and then I write for forty. But I give it treats too. I make my writer hot chocolate or get it really pretty stamps for the letters it's supposed to write. Mainly, I try to make writing feel very approachable, very daily."

My mother was a daily writer. I grew up watching her grab two minutes while the coffee brewed, ten minutes more after the breakfast dishes, sometimes while we kids practiced piano and did homework.

My mother died in 1979. A few months before her death, she came to visit me in Los Angeles. I was newly sober, newly separated from a husband I was still in love with, newly a mother, and running a rickety household in which I tried to juggle all these facts and writing. After she went home, my mother wrote me a letter. I keep that letter in a drawer in my bedroom bureau. I keep that letter in my heart. In that letter my mother said she was proud of me, she said I was running a remarkably workable household and that she was particularly pleased by my parenting. Now, my mother may have said these things over the phone to me, but what stuck was that she put it on the page. She cared enough to write it.

My mother was a great example to me about the beauty and power of writing as a palpable sign of love. She had seven children and, when we were off at school, she wrote to us. She also wrote regularly to her mother-in-law, Mimi, who wrote long and winding letters back, and to her sisters, who also wrote back often. Letters came and went from my mother's desk with the same casual flow as, yes, e-mail. My mother did not make a production out of writing. She simply did it. She did it all the time. From my mother I learned you did not need to make a Big Deal out of writing. You needed only to do it.

Doing it all the time, whether or not we are in the mood, gives us ownership of our writing ability. It takes it out of the realm of conjuring where we stand on the rock of isolation, begging the winds for inspiration, and it makes it something as do-able as picking up a hammer and pounding a nail. Writing may be an art, but it is certainly a craft. It is a simple and workable thing that can be as steady and reliable as a chore—does that ruin the romance?

My friend Richard, who lives in Venice Beach, takes a notebook out to the sand. He goes for a daily swim with the dolphins, comes back in, towels off, and sets himself to the page. The swim keeps him physically fit. The writing keeps him mentally fit. He doesn't negotiate about either practice. He doesn't wait for the "mood" for an icy plunge into the ocean or onto the page.

"I just do it," Richard says, "and I am happy when I do. Every so often I'll slip up. I'll miss writing or miss my swim, and when I do, it shows up in the rest of my life. I get irritable."

Richard, by virtue of his writing and swimming practice, is a trained optimist. Whatever mood he has to begin with becomes the building block of a better mood. "I act my way into right thinking," Richard says.

Acting our way into right thinking is putting pen to the page even when the censor is shrieking. It is choosing to write even when writing feels "wrong" to us—because we're tired, we're bothered, we're any number of things that writing will change if only we will let it. It's letting it that's the trick.

Lately, I have been talking to Regine, a beautiful, passionate young writer whose poetry comes to her in sudden visitations, arriving perfectly formed like those miracle births you read about in the tabloids. ("I didn't know I was pregnant until I delivered perfect twins!")

I have been encouraging Regine to invite her creative pregnancies, to pay attention to her stirrings, to invite the Muse to tea at regular hours to see if her writing can become a little less mysterious and more matter-of-fact.

Regine is interested by the idea of more productivity but reluctant to lose the "magic" of poems that visit like secret lovers.

Regine is like myself in the rearview mirror, in the years before I accepted my writing as a commitment, discovering it to be as committed to me as I was to it. It's a romantic notion that creativity is elusive, that it might leave at any moment like a lover whose heart flickers hot and cold.

Creativity is a lamp, not a candle. Something wants to write through us as badly as we want to write. Discovering this is a matter of time and patience.

"Just show up at the page," I advise Regine. "Put your pen to paper and begin where you are. Begin writing and something will come to you. It's like turning on a light switch. The current is there and starts to flow."

"But I hate what I write when I write that way," Regine says. "It's so self-conscious."

Regine wants to be ravaged, swept away, "taken" by her writing. I do understand. Sometimes my writing takes me like a fevered lover—yesterday, finishing a novella—and it's lovely when it does. More often, my writing and I meet halfway like a couple who want to make love amid a busy week and don't know quite how to get started.

"Love everything you write," I tell Regine. "Accept your writing as permanent, a person you are in love with who has good days and bad days, cranky days and euphoric ones. Let your writing be itself. Give it love and it will surprise you."

I explain to Regine that I take my writer out for treats, that I buy it expensive coffee concoctions with foam like clouds. I take my writer on train rides to write and admire the view. I buy my writer journals, race-along–pens, an embroidered writing chair that I place by the window with good light. I try not to bully my writer or attack it. I try not to make it write only "shoulds" without also writing "want-tos." My writer has learned to trust me, to enjoy my company, and to treat me well back.

"You know," Regine suddenly tells me one day, "some of what I write when I don't feel like writing is actually good when I look back at it later. Why is that?"

I tell Regine that moods shadow the writing landscape like passing clouds. They darken our perception of beautiful terrain and fool us into despair.

"Can they fool you the other way too?" Regine wants to know. She is young and loves looking for the leaden lining.

"I suppose so, but it's more rare and it's nothing that can't be fixed," I tell her—refusing to buy the drama.

"I hate fixing things," Regine sniffs.

"I love fixing things," I counter. "I enjoy watching my own level of craft."

"Craft!" Regine fumes at the mention of the word. She wants "Art," capital "A."

"Think of it as tricks if you want," I tell her.

Tricks like short, single-sentence paragraphs. Repetition. Dialogue in place of prose. Prose in place of dialogue. An image to break up facts. Facts to break up and ground a glistening strand of images.

"Tricks are demeaning," Regine pronounces.

"Think of it as trying different positions," I tell Regine. She is at that age where she likes anything that smacks of sex.

"You're just trying to trick me," she complains.

"Tricks work," I tell her, older and wiser. "My writing life is a little Parisian, a little decadent, arranged dates in the waning afternoon—induced moods, if you will."

"What you're really saying is just do it," Regine finally blurts out.

"Yes, I suppose I am," I tell her. "Once you start, you see, you tend to like it."

"Mmm."

"It's very hard to write without it putting you in a better mood."

"Mmm."

"I can't convince you. You just have to try it."

"I know. I know. And you're probably right!"

I am right.

My horses are staring at me through the study window. For my horses, my writing is a chore I do, something predictable. The sun comes up over the mountain, their owner gets up, drinks coffee, and writes. They see this by staring the fifteen feet from their corral to my study windows. This morning, Jack Merlin, my bright chestnut Arab named for Ed Towle's detective hero, is nibbling at grass under the fence. For the past two days he has been ambitious about getting out and eating all the bright spring shoots on my tiny patch of lawn. It's forbidden, and that's why it's attractive.

I am still writing because I am having fun doing it. This was, you'll remember, a morning when I did not want to write. My sentences were at least as cranky as my horses. Just now the sun over the mountain is gilding Carolina's particolored mane. She is preening her head over the fence, ears perked, listening. I have always thought the sound of a good typewriter reminded me of my childhood pony Chico's rapidly tapping hooves.

I did not want to write this morning. I am delighted that I have.

MOOD
Initiation   Tool

We often make the mistake of thinking that we "have" to be in the "right" mood to write. The truth is, any mood can be used for writing. Any mood is a good writing mood. The trick is to simply enter whatever mood like a room and sit down and write from there. Try this brief experiment.

Set aside fifteen minutes. Identify a situation in your life about which you have a recognizable mood or emotion. For example:

- I'm angry at my partner.
- I love the fall leaves.
- I'm sad about Mother's health.

- I'm proud of my son's schoolwork.
- I enjoy Laura's humor.
- My lover and I are getting along especially well.

Writing longhand, "enter" a mood or emotion and write for ten minutes. At the end of ten minutes, stop. Take five more minutes and write about the shifts in your mood that the act of writing caused. Be an observer: I feel happier, sadder, angrier, less angry, hopeful, determined—whatever. Write a few notes on this process, a sort of field report on your experience.

DRAMA

"KEEP THE DRAMA on the page."

I know that writers are supposed to have many physical prerequisites for practicing their craft, a room of our own being chief among them. I have had such rooms and enjoyed writing in them, but I have also done a lot of writing, more writing than in those rooms, with a notepad settled on the kitchen table, on my lap in a speeding car, or in a busy café.

Not wanting to second-guess Virginia Woolf, a woman of firm opinions, I nonetheless want to venture that she was suggesting we need a room of our own so that we could put aside the needs and agendas and dramas of others and concentrate on the actual feat of writing. In other words, she was really saying, "Keep the drama on the page."

It's a physical thing to be able to swing a door shut and put up a barrier between us and the world—or between the world and our words. As we all know, such physical barriers are only as good as they are serviceable. If we are still upset by what's going on on the far side of the door, we will still have a hard time writing. The trick is, therefore, a psychological door, not a physical one—a door that is really proof against the intrusions of others and their agendas.

I wrote many movies with my daughter Domenica crawling and

then toddling underfoot. I answered phones, changed diapers, si-lenced squalls, patted brows, admired doll clothes, organized dress-ups, and kept writing. In other words, I stayed knee-deep in both the flow of life and the flow of words.

How did I do that?

I made a deal with myself. The deal was: Keep the drama on the page.

This deal, simple in the statement, is the key to all serenity and accomplishment as a writer. It's a habit of saying, when drama rears its head, "I'll think about that later—after I write."

As I write this, two of my closest friends in all the world are fighting. Both sides are phoning me regularly with grievances and ul-timatums. I am saying, "Mmm. Let's not escalate all this. Mmm. Re-member you both have a lot of integrity."

That's what I am saying to them—and calmly, sweetly. I am like the peacemaker from a Jane Austen novel. This is all very good news. "Don't forget you love each other. You used to and you still really do. This will blow over," I say.

That is all I say: immaculate detachment, no sides chosen.

Is this because I am St. Julia?

Hardly. To myself I say, "You idiots. Do something else besides feud. For example, why not write something?"

Hearing "Why not write something," I come to my desk and I write. I write despite the fact that my best friends are feuding. I write despite escalating lawyers' letters zipping like paper airplanes. I write because I have a rule, and that is "Keep the drama on the page."

It could be argued that I am ruthless. It is a well-earned ruthless-ness. I have learned through bitter experience that if I start engaging in personal dramas, I will be too tired, too distracted, too distraught to write—and I cannot afford that.

For a writer, personal drama is a drink of creative poison. For a writer, the willing engagement in power struggles is an act of active creative sabotage.

"But he!" shouts one of my friends.

"But she!" shouts the other.

I, meanwhile, pick my way carefully through the center.

"I can't really get into this now. I'm sure you'll work it out. I'm due at the page."

And I am "due" at the page. That term, with its hint of pregnancy and gestation, is another thing I have learned. Every day is made from myriad moments. In each of these moments we have choices:

Will I write for twenty minutes or spend twenty minutes on the phone playing wailing wall?

Will I walk the dogs for twenty minutes and use that time to mull story lines, or will I tell myself I don't have time for walking and call my sister to complain about how my life is not my own?

Will I keep the drama on the page, in other words, or will I engage in a drama that will keep me from the page?

One of my favorite movies is *Twentieth Century*. In it, John Barrymore plays a ruthless theatrical impresario. Whenever he is crossed by someone whose will seeks to thwart his own, Barrymore hisses, "That rat . . . I slam the iron door."

Once he has slammed the Iron Door, the person or problem no longer exists for Mr. Barrymore. What does exist is whatever theatrical problem he was wrestling with. In other words, his is a ruthless, enlightened self-interest.

Keeping the drama on the page is ruthless, enlightened self-interest. It is a practice of creative self-containment that makes the luxury of a room of one's own largely a matter of convenience, not necessity.

"She's got forty-eight hours to apologize to me or else . . ."

"I'm sure it will work out. You're both adults."

"She's not!"

"He's not."

"Hmmm. I am due at the page."

With that, I head back to the blank sheet of paper. I slam the Iron Door. I refuse to engage in any drama except the drama that serves me and my purposes. I practice exactly what I preach: if you dump drama into my life, I will put it and you onto the page.

DRAMA
Initiation Tool

Drama in our lives often keeps us from putting drama on the page. Some drama happens and we lose our sense of scale in our emotional landscape. When this happens, we need to reconnect to our emotional through line. We need a sense of our "before, during, and after life." This tool is a personal antidote for too much drama.

Set aside one half hour. Settle yourself comfortably. Number from one to a hundred. Now list one hundred things you, personally, love. For example:

1. Raspberries
2. Peonies
3. New York pizza
4. The scent of pine
5. Needlepoint pillows
6. Rumi poetry
7. Mack semitrailer trucks
8. Key lime pie
9. Maria Callas
10. Rhubarb
11. Shubert's "Ave Maria"
12. Handel's *Messiah*
13. Emmylou Harris
14. Flying
15. Horses, especially palominos

Keep a copy of the list in your wallet or desk drawer. When stress strikes, read the list. It will instantly connect you to a sense of well-being apart from the current drama.

THE WALL OF INFAMY

LET ME SHOW you how I use drama.

When I was in the throes of a public Hollywood divorce, I was stunned to receive in the mail clippings from "friends" across the country regarding news stories on my adulterous spouse. My newly famous husband had run off with my very famous friend. Why would I want to read about it?

Was this "any news is good news" thinking? Was this "just spell my name right" thinking? What it felt like was sadism. Don't people realize that fame is no talisman against human pain? Adultery is still adultery.

The word "clipping" began to take on a new and ominous tone. More than my wings—my heart, my pride, and, if I'd been a man, I'd have said something else—was getting clipped.

"The spurned, cuckolded wife"—what a self-image! And there it was in black and white.

But I saw red.

Forget "They cannot do this to me." They had done it. The real question was "What was I going to do about it?" How would I "right" things? I would write things, I decided. Specifically, I would write a movie about all the themes twisting through my life: love, friendship, treachery, and revenge. To help me in this endeavor, I invented a new writing tool: The Wall of Infamy.

Rather than burn the clippings, toss the clippings, or bury them in a drawer and try to forget or ignore the clippings, I reminded myself that emotion was fuel and I might as well use my hurt feelings to write. My "writing station" at that time was a small eighteenth-century desk facing out over a garden. The desk sat in front of long French windows. The windows had muslin curtains which I used to pin the clippings on. I would sit down to write, feel overwhelmed by pain, and think to myself, "I cannot do this. I cannot survive this pain."

"Oh, yes, you can," another little voice would tell me. "Write right at them! Don't let the bastards get you down."

When this voice whispered that I could keep writing, I would glance up at the clippings: my husband dancing with his new love— my supposed friend. At the sight of them cheek to cheek, adrenaline would fly straight to my fingers. The smoldering anger and resentment became the ashes for a phoenix to rise from. A day at a time, a page at a time, a glance at a time at my Wall of Infamy and my script pages piled up. Days after the script was finished, my agent sold the script to Paramount. In my case, the Wall of Infamy literally spelled "curtains" to my former life.

Like me, you can use your negative feelings as positive fuel. While my script was grounded in the pain and anger of betrayal, it soon took on other colors, other questions. Characters that begin with a base in a real person soon enough become characters in their own rights, citizens with their own opinions, denizens of a world that very rapidly seems to be more about their making than my own. In other words, writing for revenge, writing to "show them," is a perfectly fine way to start, because sooner or later what you show yourself is the willingness and invention of your own creativity. It is difficult, almost impossible, to stay mired in the details of actual autobiographical experience as alternate routings come to mind and pen.

My friend Trent is a political writer. His books are long, intricate explorations of the machinations of power between the haves and the have-nots. As a writer, Trent is a soldier. He shows up day after day, year after year, marshaling his resources to continue the good fight. Trent is unstoppable as a writer—and part of what fuels him is his version of the Wall of Infamy.

Trent keeps clipping files of everything he reads that outrages him and fires his social conscience. The files—updated constantly—are the prods Trent uses when his energies lag. Opening a file whenever his writing energies wane, he reads a little and then returns to the page freshly energized by his outrage at social injustice.

In the throes of a hellish, high-drama divorce, Howard, a screenwriter, wrote about it. His estranged wife emerged on the page vivid as real life with a few chivalrous changes: height, weight, hair color. The script wrought from Howard's divorce is one of the funniest I've ever read. The pain he encountered in life became painfully funny on the page.

"My ten-million-dollar home movie," a film director I know refers to his own forged-from-the-annals-of-hell relationship drama. Oscar-nominated, as I recall.

So, yes, I advocate writing for revenge. I advocate writing "to show them." You turn the dross of your disappointments into the gold of accomplishment. In the long run, the person you show is yourself.

THE WALL OF INFAMY
Initiation Tool

When injuries are buried instead of acknowledged, they create a potent writer's block. Lurking in our unconscious, they "mysteriously" leech us of writing power. Made conscious, our creative villains can be actively faced down. This tool allows you to learn the knack of writing "at" your creative villains. It aims at helping you identify characters for your Wall of Infamy and giving you a strategem for dealing with their imapct.

Step one: Set aside one half hour. Number from one to three. Casting back over your life, list three people who have been for you "creative monsters," that is, people who have criticized, undercut, or sabotaged your creativity.

1.

2.

3.

Number from one to three again. Now list three people you'd like to "show." (Some of the names from both lists may be the same.)

1.

2.

3.

Step two: Write out the following sentences, using your name.

1.   I, (name), am able to achieve success despite my creative monsters' opinions.

2.   I, (name), am able to release (name), (name), and (name) to their destiny. I am able to successfully claim my own.

3.   I, (name), am able to use my anger by focusing it to write my way clear of rage, frustration, and negativity.

You may wish to "post" this declaration of independence—or even tape it inside a desk drawer.

VALUING OUR EXPERIENCE

W_E DO NOT see our size. We do not view ourselves with accuracy. We are far larger, far more marvelous, far more deeply and consistently creative than we recognize or know.

We do not credit ourselves with what it is we can—and often do—accomplish. We are blind to our gifts; we are deaf to our voice. We do not see or hear our magnitude. Why is this?

Seeking to value ourselves, we look to others for assurance. If what we are doing threatens them, they cannot give it. If what we envision is larger than what they can see, they cannot give support for what it is we are doing.

When people cannot see the larger picture of what it is we are trying to do, they will pick out some detail and pick at that. We have, many of us, had the experience of being all dressed up, ready to go somewhere and feeling pretty marvelous, when someone—a parent, a friend, even the baby-sitter—picks a small piece of lint off our outfit. "Lint picking" is focusing on the small imperfection rather than seeing the greater glory of the whole.

As writers, as artists, we are often confronted with lint pickers. Most teachers—not all, but most—are lint pickers when they grade papers. All grammatical errors are clearly marked in red, but where is the sentence that says, "This phrase is great! The overall thinking here is marvelous"? Most of us never got that kind of feedback, and we don't get it still.

This morning I talked to a young playwright who had just written a marvelous play and directed it as well for a chance to see it on its feet. The play is a marvelous, tough-minded, brilliant piece of work. The direction was nimble, accurate, and appropriate. The feedback from the playwright's jealous peers? Mainly lint picking. How is the playwright to understand the size of what's been done when the comments all address the creative lint? In other words, how do we stay both small enough and big enough to create?

We must be small enough, humble enough, to always be a beginner, an observer. We must be open to experience, new experience, new sources of knowledge and insight, while still staying grounded in the fact that what we already know and have done is also estimable, also important. In short, we must stay big enough to recognize that any individual criticism, any negative feedback, accurate or not, must always be seen in light of the bigger picture: we have actually made something and we plan to make many—and perhaps better—things more. In other words, how do we stay vulnerable enough to and tough enough to survive?

Part of the answer is what people often, erroneously, call "discipline." What a thankless word that is—and how beside the point. What a better word, or thought, the term "routine" is. We need to establish a creative routine, a rote, do-able, daily something that is there to fall back on. For me, I write three pages of longhand every morning. It doesn't take me long, but it takes me far. After I finish that, after I feed and water my horses and, for that matter, myself, I sit down and I write a couple of pages of something more.

It is one of the ironies of the writing life that much of what we write in passing, casually, later seems to hold up just as well as the pieces we slaved over, convinced of their worth and dignity.

Ease and difficulty of writing have little to do, in the long run, with the quality of what gets produced. A "bad" writing day can produce good writing. A "good" writing day can produce something we later feel needs a substantial rewrite to make the grade. The point is to value all of what we write, to learn not to be swayed by the mood of the moment into hasty judgments. Too many times, torn-up pages are merely a reflection of our mood and not a reflection of merit.

The computer, with its deadly "delete" button, should be seen as a clear and present enemy. Most often, a small scrap of writing that we are tempted to send to oblivion can be saved in a "slush" file and found to fit perfectly later.

"I'm often astounded by what I write in passing without even noticing it in my journal," Alex told me. "I was ready to pitch all my journals because they were just building up, when I decided to look back through them first. I was astounded. There were all sorts of great ideas and some really great fragments. I think, on the one hand, it is good to write so casually that I can just toss writing off. On the other hand, I don't want to be so casual that I just toss writing away."

I have been writing Morning Pages for the better part of two decades. While they are not intended to be art, they are often a seed for art. My musical *Avalon* began as a single sentence, a tease: "Wouldn't it be fun to write a musical about Merlin." Countless students have told me their own creative adventures began with similar one-line asides, sudden insights they set to the page. Kathy, a musician, was mid-album when her pages suggested a shift in direction more true to herself. The resulting album was considered to be "breakthrough" work—work that came about because Kathy, through daily writing, had learned to value her experience.

Valuing our experience is not narcissism. It is not endless self-involvement. It is, rather, the act of paying active witness to ourselves and to our world. Such witness is an act of dignity, an act that recognizes that life is essentially a sacred transaction of which we know only the shadow, not the shape. As we attune ourselves more and more closely to the value of passing moments, we learn that we are something of moment ourselves.

Valuing Our Experience
Initiation Tool

Writing is an act of self-cherishing. We often write most deeply and happily on those areas closest to our heart. This tool contains clues to your personal value system. Set aside one hour. Take yourself out of the house and to a pleasant writing environment. It could be a coffee shop, but it could be a church, synagogue, or library. Number from one to fifty. List fifty things you are proud of, from the small to the large, for example:

1. Moving to New York
2. Writing a one-act play
3. Giving up alcohol
4. Remembering our anniversary
5. Putting myself through college
6. My pie crust
7. My rapport with dogs
8. My relationship with my mother
9. The design I did for our newsletter
10. Losing the ten pounds and keeping it off

During the next week, review this list several times at your leisure. What does it teach you about what you value? You may find you value your sense of daring, or your sense of thoughtfulness, physical adventures or intellectual ones, acts of outer initiative or times of inner reflection. Knowing what experiences have been important to you is a clue not only to what you might want to do more of but also to what you might want to write about.

SPECIFICITY

I BELIEVE IN SPECIFICITY. I trust it. Specificity is like breathing: one breath at a time, that is how life is built. One thing at a time, one thought, one word at a time. That is how a writing life is built.

Writing is about living. It is about specificity. Writing is about seeing, hearing, feeling, smelling, touching. It is more about all these things than it is about thinking. We have an idea that "writers" must be "smart." By smart, we actually mean "clever." We know what clever looks like, it is the Maserati turn of a phrase, the cornering of a comment with a speed and grace the rest of us can't handle. Yes, that's one form of writing, the showy kind, but that is not all that writing is about.

Go back to the breath, to the way that it sustains us. We do not have to think about it. When we try to, it can be hard, then easy, then interesting, then calm, safe, centering. Writing, when we let ourselves do it, is like breathing. It doesn't have to be fancy. It need only be regular and steady. That is deep enough. That takes us deeper.

And how, then, do we go deeper? Writing regularly and steadily, we strive to be specific. We focus on our writing the way, as a mediator, we focus on our breath. We "notice" the precise word that occurs to us. We use that word and then we "notice" another word. It is a listening process, a focusing on what rises up so we can take it down.

I love to write in the mornings, but I am writing this midway through Mother's Day, a long afternoon. Outside my study window, birds are insistently chirping—now they've stopped. There is a magpie nest in a smallish tree. It is a big nest, not stable-looking, and I worry about it during storms. Then I think, "Those magpies know what they're doing. It's what they do."

If we let ourselves write, we also come to know what we're doing. We know how to write because writing is what we do. The more we do it, the more specifically and regularly we do it, the easier it is to do: like hammering a nail, you get the swing of it when you do it more often than Sunday repairs.

For many of us, writing has been reserved for Sunday repairs. We "repair" to the page (there's a writerly bit of cornering) to examine some sharp pain, to see if we can express an extreme emotion: anger, passion, resentment, a proposal, love—especially love. Love letters exist as a genre because the force of our emotions forces us to write. "I don't know how to tell you," we write. . . .

But we do know how to tell. We know if we will let ourselves know. We know if we are willing to be specific.

Being specific in writing means taking the general and looking at it more closely. "I feel OK about that" then becomes "I don't feel good about that, but I do not feel so terrible either. I feel disappointed and resigned. I am close to depression, which I hope will pass."

Sometimes, often, specificity is as simple as facts. "A horse" becomes "a small brown horse with a white star and a wispy tail." Each fact adds to our credibility. The reader trusts us because we give enough detail for our eyes—which they are using—to be trusted.

Sensual specificity is another way to get specific. "Cold" or "hot." "Bright" or "dark." "Sweet-smelling" or "rank." Our senses give readers a "sense" of what we are writing about.

Sometimes specificity is tonal. A room is "proper" or "cozy." A lover's voice is "welcoming" or "chill." A sky is sunny and "expansive" or "foreboding."

Sometimes specificity shows in our verbs. A boat "skims" or "slices" the water. A cat "leaps" or "pounces." A phone "rings" or "shrills."

Writing is making choices, and the choices we make can be

generic, which will cost us our reader's faith, or specific, which will gain our reader's trust. Detail allows us to communicate precisely what we mean.

For me, part of the ability to be specific has to do with writing to a specific someone, someone who "gets you." I know that writers are often told not to think about their audience, but I think that advice can be difficult to use. The audience then becomes something vague and amorphous. How do you communicate with that? And isn't ignoring it just a little coy?

Better to let the audience be someone real—a lover, a best friend, a colleague, someone who gets your jokes or just likes how you think. Choose someone on whom nothing will be wasted, someone with an appetite for life in all its messy glory. That someone will enjoy your writing specifically. Write specifically to that someone. This will make your writing targeted and focused. It will also bring to your writing a purity of intent.

In the practice of singing, much can be done with technique. There is, however, an elusive something that comes when the singer "sings with love." That intention brings to the voice a purity that is at once evanescent and unmistakable. The same purification happens to our writing when we write with specific loving intent. It is a great paradox that the more personal, focused, and specific your writing becomes, the more universally it communicates.

Although we seldom view it this way, specificity is freedom. In the act of naming things precisely as they appear to us, we free our work from misunderstandings, from ambiguity, from vagueness. At its base, writing is an act of love, and when we perform it consciously, concretely, and lovingly, grace enters the equation. We—and the reader—have an experience of something larger communicating through the vessel of our work. That larger something—whose eye is on the sparrow—knows a great deal about the value of specificity.

"God is in the details," exclaimed Ludwig Mies van der Rohe. Writing specifically, writing detail by detail, we encounter not only ourselves, not only our truth, but the greater truth that stands behind all art and all communication. We touch the spiritual fact that as divided as we may feel ourselves to be, we are nonetheless One. That is the central fact that all real writing communicates—and it does it specifically.

AFTER RAIN IN TAOS VALLEY

The clouds graze like great mammals
Nibbling the hills.
They are white, woolly, tender
And large enough to eat me.

SPECIFICITY
Initiation Tool

Although we tend to think of it as linear, writing is a profoundly visual art. Even if we are writing about internal experience, we use images to do it. For this reason, we must consciously and constantly restock our store of images. We do this by focusing on what is around us. This tool is not intended to be high art or serious writing. It is simply an exercise in observation.

Set aside one hour. Settle in to write at home or "out." Begin by numbering from one to ten. List and describe ten items in your immediate environment. What are your associations with them, however nonsensical. For example:

1.   A silver espresso machine. Its intricate gadgetry reminds me of the movie *Metropolis.*
2.   A smoked mirror. I associate these with brothels, salons, and sexual decadence.
3.   A white-shirted waitress. I connect to a sense of sweetness and life at a slower pace. I am reminded of Edward Hopper paintings, pulp novels like *The Postman Always Rings Twice.*

Now, step two: List and describe ten personal objects that have for you personal emotional weight. Describe especially both the object and the reasons for its emotional relevance.

1.   A vintage poster of circus acrobats. This I connect to my memories of my father and his later life on Long Boat Key near the Ringling Brothers winter quarters.

2.   A blue and white porcelain Chinese jar, twined with dragons. My "God jar." Bought in Chinatown, Los Angeles, in the late seventies, when I was newly sober and needed help with my many worries. I would place a worry into the jar and later see its outworking as an answered prayer.

3.   A stone carving of a mother owl cradling her young. This is for me an image of the mysterious and protective higher forces at play in my life.

Connecting to our environment consciously and concretely allows us to connect with greater specificity and emotional resonance to our own inner life. This makes for writing of a rich timbre.

BODY OF EXPERIENCE

We often talk about a writer having "a body of work" without realizing that this is a literal phrase. Because we think of writing as something disembodied and cerebral, because we "think" of writing rather than notice that what we do with it is really meet or encounter it, we seldom realize that writing, like all art, is an embodied experience.

When I have a tangled plot line, I walk to sort it out. I walk and I mull. I am not exactly "thinking" about my writing as I walk, but the question is there, posed by my mind to my body. My body, which carries a knowledge deeper than my mind, has answers for me as an artist and as a person. My mind, anyone's mind, for all its multifaceted brilliance, can be a house of mirrors, a maze of dead ends when seeking a creative solution.

Composer Michael Hoppe goes running daily to catch his melody lines. The songlines he seeks snake through Los Angeles as they snake through all of our green planet. We can feel them if we will enter our bodies and actively seek them out. Hoppe seeks melody through his long, loping runs. Melodies occur a note at a time, just like writing.

My friend Natalie Goldberg, both writer and painter, sets herself long hikes through the sagebrush. She lets the landscape speak to her questions. My friend John Nichols, writer, photographer, and ecologist, hikes a small mountain every afternoon at twilight. He climbs, and the work of climbing puts him into his body and into his body of work. Home from his hike, he writes evening into dawn. That is his work "day."

For myself, when I am writing music, melody and lyrics, I love to roller-skate. The summer I lived in London, writing my musical *Avalon,* I took daily, sometimes twice daily, forays to Regents Park. There, amid the canals on which the "queen's swans" glided, I sang my lyrics into a handheld tape recorder while my skates—stroke, stroke, stroke, just like a pen—did the work of writing for me.

We look at the fact that the British nature poets were great walkers, but we seldom make the connection that poetry is comprised of "feet" and that walking was a part of the poets' creative path. We read Robert Frost without realizing how pivotal walking was to his writing life: "Two roads diverged in a wood."

That wood was not something he sped by in a car. Frost's woods, his tumbledown stone walls, his birches—in short, the images and insights that comprise his most-known body of work—these came to him at eye level. His poetic feet actually walked the earth.

We store memories in our bodies. We store passion and heartache. We store joy, moments of transcendent peace. If we are to access these, if we are to move into them and through them, we must enter our bodies to do so. When we encounter an emotional shock, the trauma of a lost beloved, the grief of separation, our bodies count the cost. Our minds may go numb, adroit at denial, but our bodies hold fast to the truth.

Entering our bodies, we enter our hearts. "Heart" is where the "art" is. This is why writing by hand, even when it seems clumsy and inconvenient, can lead us to a deeper truth than our flying fingers at the keys. We are "sentenced" to a life in our bodies. That, too, is a telling phrase.

Our bodies are storytellers. To test this, lie on a massage table with music like Michael Hoppe's "The Yearning" gently unspooling in the background. As the therapist kneads your body, your body will speak to you. It will tell you your own needs. It will tell you the cost of your life as well as what is priceless to you. Images and memories will arise at the touch of a finger. Muscles will unlock to whisper your pains and your dreams.

Yes, we have a body of work, and to enter it fully we must enter our bodies. This is true for all of us. Proust, imprisoned by infirmity, remains a profoundly sensual writer. Our bodies are something more than the cage for our minds. Our bodies are the vehicles of our self-expression. Our eyes, ears, lips, tongue, back, shoulders, thighs, private parts—all of these are writing implements. We speak of "parts of speech." That, too, is another telling phrase.

When writing sours from too much writing, a longish walk can sweeten it again. As the estimable writing teacher Brenda Ueland writes, "I will tell you what I have learned myself. For me, a long five- or six-mile walk helps. And one must go alone and every day."

When I have a shock, I walk to metabolize it. Walking, seeking only to move and in moving "move" something through, I often come to an entirely unexpected idea. I happen upon it with the same delighted shock that I have when my woodland walking brings me unexpectedly up upon a deer. "Oh! Look at that!" I think, creeping closer to the thought to examine it.

"Before I compose a piece, I walk around it several times, accompanied by myself," remarked composer Eric Satie. A piece of writing, like a piece of music, benefits from the same physical exploration.

I notice that in writing about physicality in writing, I have opened the door to composers to say their bit. This is not coincidental. We "compose" a letter. We "take notes" before we write. We talk about the "musicality" of someone's "flowing" prose. Is it any surprise that composers have lessons to teach us and that the lessons they teach us relate to our having a body of work?

"I learn by going where I have to go," wrote poet Theodore Roethke. He was another great walker. Walking, we encounter a timeless dimension, a realm beyond time in which experience is acute and ancient. Composer Tim Wheater named one of his albums *Timeless*. It is a paean to this imaginative realm. I have a poem about the body and the fact that it embodies far more wisdom, more spiritual DNA, than we normally acknowledge. Our ancestors and our ancestral wisdom live in our blood and in our bones.

THE QUIET ANIMAL

O quiet animal, sleeping,
What dreams lie within your cells?
What ages brought you here
Through coal and ice?
Eye twitch, lip curl—
Blood dreams again.

Blood is always dreaming.
Scheming to move us forward and take us back,
Dreaming the dark places,
Caves and the backs of stars.

Your ivory bones are the tusks of time
Who eats with all our mouths.
That crescent moon? It's just a bone
Thrown beyond our reach.
The stars at night were someone's baby teeth.

The blood remembers
What the mind forgets.
The soul is a quiet animal.
Given less to thought than memory,
More to dreams than plan,
The soul owes more to half-remembered God
Than waking life as man.

When we "reach" for a word in our writing, we need to reach inward, not outward. The body has the word for us if we will just listen to what it volunteers. Touch is incredibly precise, delicate, and powerful; we say we want our writing to "touch" people, but we seldom look at the fact that in order to do so it must embody our actual experience. Our language must be physical. This is how we "touch" our reader.

We speak of writing "having energy" and again, we do not look

at the literalness of that phrase. Writes spiritual teacher
quette: "The power of the word is real whether or not
scious of it. . . . Behind every word flows energy."

I recently had an uncanny experience. I met a very precise, heart-
centered writer—but I did not know that this was the case. I met this
man and as we were crossing a busy Manhattan street, he touched me
once, gently, in the center of my back. Instantly, I felt safe, protected,
and understood. I thought, "What a lovely energy this man has."

Reading this man later, I found that same energy—recognizable,
deft, precise, delicate, and powerful—running through his prose. It
"touched" me. It touched me as surely, as deliberately, and as physically as he had himself. We speak of someone's writing having a "nice
touch," but again we think of it solely as metaphor. It is not mere
metaphor.

Victoria, a young writer, is in love with Peter, another young
writer. They communicate near daily across the Atlantic by fax.
Watching her, watching the old-fashioned relationship that is unfolding a day at a time, a page at a time, just as it did in Victorian England,
I see the wisdom and the strength that come from a relationship that
is not raced through pell-mell but instead constructed a word at a
time, a thought at a time. I have seen Victoria after a long and literate
fax from Peter. She glows like a woman who has just been kissed.
Peter's writing touches her.

"Reach out and touch somebody," AT&T advertising urges us.
How much more thoroughly we can touch if we write!

We must "embody" our truth, spiritual teachers tell us. What
they don't often tell us is that we already do. If we are only half in our
bodies, we are only half in our truth. If we separate our body, mind,
and spirit into three separate components, three distinct elements and
compartments, we are hacking up our body of experience. As writers,
we are dismembering or, even more accurately, "dis-remembering"
ourselves.

For several centuries now, in the West, we have engaged or in-
dulged in an expensive dualism in which body and mind are separate
and mind is ascendant. The mind, disembodied, divorced from the
heart, can rationalize atrocity: the ultimate solution can seem, on

paper, like a good idea. It did to a number of people. If we continue to divorce our hearts from our art, it could again.

The word "conscience" has two parts to it: "con" (with) and "science" (knowing). We cannot have a conscience when we dismember our body of work from our body. We must allow our selves to be "with" the "knowing" that our body has to offer. This is why it is called not only a "body of work" but a "body of knowledge." True knowledge, authentic knowledge, is something deeper than the mind entertains.

The poet Pablo Neruda made from the body of his beloved a body of work that is universal because of its specificity. Reading him, I always feel the words first in my heart; only later do they march across my mind. Another poem of mine, a linguistics lesson learned by loving Neruda:

BODY ENGLISH

We speak in tongues.
My mouth to your ear.
Your ear to my mouth.
We speak in tongues,
Use body English.
Mouth to mouth.
Heart to heart.
Parts of speech.
Each.
Our every slip of the tongue is graceful.
Our best syllables are silent.
We speak in tongues.
Our skins make conversation.
Talk to me.

BODY OF EXPERIENCE
Initiation Tool

Writing is a physical as well as a psychological act. Many of our most marvelous writers have been great walkers. There is something about the rhythm of the walk. There is a musicality in motion that spills onto the page.

Set aside one half hour. Put on comfortable shoes and walking clothes. You may wish to choose a specific question, query, or topic to take on your walk. You may choose to ask instead for "whatever I need to know." Head out the door and walk for twenty minutes. Notice your surroundings. Notice your mood. Notice any shifts in your mood. Above all, notice any answers, insights, stratagems, or inspirations that come to you. Back home, head directly to the page. Record your experience and your findings.

The Well

As WRITERS, WE DRAW on an inner fund of images that I call "the well." I think of this well like an inner pond, one that must be kept both stocked and freely flowing. Thinking of this inner reservoir as an ecosystem answers some often baffling writer's questions, chief among them: "Why is the work drying up just when it was going so well?"

Very often work dries up precisely because it was going so well. We have simply overfished our inner reservoir without having taken the time and care to consciously restock our storehouse of images.

The device I use to restock the pond is a very simple one, something which I call an "Artist Date." Put simply, an Artist Date is a once-weekly solitary expedition to something festive that interests us. It can be a visit to a museum, an aquarium store, a yarn shop. It can be a concert, a movie, an exhibition on dinosaurs. The point is to go somewhere fascinating and to go there alone.

Why alone?

We go alone because an Artist Date is half "artist" and half "date." You are romancing, wooing, courting your creative consciousness. This is something that requires you and your inner artist to spend time alone. For many of us, the idea of a solitary expedition brings up instant resistance.

"I'm alone all the time anyway."

"What will I tell my boyfriend?"

"Who is going to watch the kids?"

Such resistance is normal, but it is exactly that: resistance. Resisting our resistance makes us stronger. Taking the time and care to restock our inner well makes writing a far easier proposition. We are no longer fishing in vain trying to hook images that are few and far between and elusive. Instead, we are fishing into an inner reservoir that is richly stocked, one teeming with images and ideas that are ready and waiting for us to hook them.

Writing is done in black and white, but in order to be done well, it must be done colorfully. If we lead chaotic lives, it is difficult to write smoothly and steadily. If, on the other hand, we lead lives that are too regular, too sterile, our voice as writers will also go flat, leaving us straining for effect in an attempt to manufacture interest.

One of the mysteries of the writing life is the fact that an investment of interest in column A—let us say, listening to a great piece of music—will pay off obliquely when we set pen to paper on an entirely different topic. We can perhaps understand the value of doing reading and research directly connected to a piece of work, but we have a harder time seeing the value of self-enrichment simply for its own sake. We want our cause and effect to be more linear, but writing rarely works like that.

Writing is what we make from the broth of our experience. If we lead a rich and varied life, we will have a rich and varied stock of ingredients from which to draw on. If we lead a life that is too narrow, too focused, too oriented toward our goals, we will find our writing lacks flavor, is thin on the nutrients that make it both savory and sustaining.

When we are writing regularly and steadily, a once-a-week expedition is a good amount of writerly upkeep. When we are writing heavily and intensely, twice-a-week expeditions are to be recommended. It is, of course, a paradox that at no time will you feel less like restocking the well than when the writing is flowing easily and well.

"Not now! I'm writing," we are tempted to say, wanting to stick with the flow of what we are doing.

This temptation to hibernate and binge on our writing is a tendency that works in the short term but not in the long term. As one wag put it, "It's OK for the single but not for the album."

If we are invested in a writing life—as opposed to a writing career—then we are in it for the process and not the product. We are in it for the body of work and not for the quick hit of one well-realized piece. This means we must treat ourselves as valued athletes who must be kept in condition and not overraced or overtrained.

Thinking of a writing life like an athletic career, one comes to the wisdom that marathon runners know very well: ten slow miles are necessary to balance every one fast mile. Stretching is necessary to keep the body limber after and before a long run.

So, too, as writers, care and maintenance of our writing muscles are necessary for our writing stamina. This means that we must take the time and attention necessary to fill the well instead of drawing on it unrelentingly and without consciousness of our inner limits. While this may sound difficult or onerous, the payoff in terms of our writing lives is enormous. Even the smallest amount of self-nurturance will have an immediate and beneficial impact on our writing. A regular and gentle program of self-care will result in a level of ease and authority in our writing that is often astounding.

"I had begun to feel stale and exhausted," Casey, a fiction writer, told me. "I'd been writing so well that I was really happy and then suddenly everything began to feel flat and stale. I found myself bored and felt myself boring. Writing became very uphill. My stubbornness told me I needed to dig in and flog myself to produce more writing. Fortunately, I suddenly remembered Artist Dates and when I took one, sanity began to return."

Sanity in writing means writing with relative ease and fluidity. It means writing from a full well and not an empty one. Sanity in writing means acknowledging that we are a creative ecosystem and that without fresh inflow and steady outflow the pond of our inner resources can grow stagnant and stale.

"I was midway across a longish project when my writing dried up," Annie, a nonfiction writer, told me. "I had been sailing along in love with my work, when I got struck by a bad cold and was housebound for a week. Housebound, I kept right on writing. What I did not do was take any action to replenish the inner well. I wrote and wrote and wrote and suddenly it felt like I couldn't write another word." She had overfished the pond.

Fortunately Annie was a seasoned writer who was able to diagnose her spiritual malaise. Still housebound, she borrowed a set of classical music tapes and allowed herself to replenish the well through listening.

"I couldn't get out of bed, but I could change my mental scenery. I listened to Schubert's 'Ave Maria,' and as I did I felt a fresh flow of energy and inspiration. I let the music wash over me, and after an hour or so of listening I felt invigorated and refreshed. I was able to write again, but I made it a point until I got well to listen to an hour of music a day."

Karen, living in midtown Manhattan, found herself stalled out halfway through a play. Like Annie, she had been writing well but too hard.

"I felt lifeless so I put myself on a diet of life. I took myself to every plant and pet store in my neighborhood. I let myself admire orchids, enjoy cacti, ogle an amaryllis, and visit with several sets of cockatoos. All I took home was a single African violet, but my spirit revived and I returned to my writing revitalized. I am always surprised by how little it takes to revive my writing spirits."

Even better than reviving our writing spirits is maintaining the habit of renewing them. Regular Artist Dates, like regular exercise, allow us to maintain both our stamina and our tone.

THE WELL
Initiation Tool

This tool is one I traditionally call an "Artist Date." Learning to take such dates is pivotal to artistic maintenance. They enrich a sense of well-being and create a bubbling up of inspiration and insight. This will spill onto the page.

Set aside one hour. Get out of the house, off your beaten path, and do something festive and adventurous. Do it *alone*. Aim for a sensory experience. Think mystery, not mastery. Choose an activity that appeals to what you might call your inner artist, inner child, or inner explorer. Remember: What you are doing is called an "Artist Date," equal parts "artist" and "date." Do something fascinating and do not stand yourself up. You might:

1. Visit an aquarium
2. Go to a plant store
3. Visit a cathedral
4. Go to a jazz club
5. Go to a fabric store
6. Visit a gallery
7. Go to a map store
8. Visit a museum
9. Go to a vintage film
10. Visit a botanical garden

Whatever you choose to do, do it solo. Allow yourself to soak up images and impressions. No need to write about them. You are to fill the well, not fish from it.

SKETCHING

IT IS A CRYSTALLINE day, actively warm and bright. The apple blossoms are holding, full and plump. The lilacs are budding, close to bloom. A protective leafy branch now covers the front of the wren house. All of this reminds me of writing.

When I sketch in a piece, I draw the tree branch but the leaves come later. I draw the lilac bush but its bloom and scent come at a later point. I draw the apple tree but the pale pink lace is an added filigree later. In other words, I trust the writing that writes through me. I let it sketch through me. And "sketch" is the operative word.

If I see or hear the impulse to put in a tree, I put it in the landscape of what I am writing. At first it is just a little stick tree. I do not need to know why it is going in or what purpose it will serve. If I just obediently put it in—the "sketch" of a tree—the writing itself knows when and how and where it will use it.

You might call what I practice here "learned faith." I did not always know that the writing knew what it was doing. Long years of experience have taught me this is true. It is the experience of trusting—and having that trust rewarded—that makes me feel trust is appropriate. It is also the experience of having not trusted—only to come back later after much work to the original impulse—that makes me know that there is something surefooted in the creative impulses exactly as they arise.

When I was a full-time screenwriter, I was happy for a long time just writing down the movies I saw in my head. Then the screenwriting books came out, and with them the suggestion that movies be planned, broken into acts, "constructed" according to plot points. This made the writing of a movie less like a road trip and more like connecting the dots. I had always written scripts by simply telling the story as it unspooled before me. (I sold nine scripts in a row written this way.) It was a lot like getting in a car in New York and driving to California: I knew where to start and where to end and that Chicago was somewhere in the middle, the Rockies somewhere after that, but, beyond that, it was all adventure.

Now, according to the screenwriting books—which function for a writer not unlike calling Triple A for planning a road trip—I was supposed to be aiming for a certain motel my third night out. What was the fun in that? Where were the back roads, the chance to dally, the lure of unexpected roadside attractions like the pony express station midway across Kansas? Were those to be ignored? And besides, if I could figure out ahead of time what was going to happen, wouldn't the viewer be able to do exactly the same thing? Didn't "the logical next scene" bear an alarming resemblance to the "predictable next scene"? I thought so, and so I tried to shake off the advice the books offered or reserve the use of it for second drafts.

Maybe I was just stubborn—or maybe I had had too many experiences of the writing knowing more on an unconscious level than I ever knew consciously.

Ten pages into a certain script, a gun showed up on a kitchen table. "What's that doing here?" I wondered. "Why is this gun being dropped into my heroine's kitchen? She doesn't need a gun. It's not that kind of a movie. Oh, well, it's here, so I'll leave it in, but it's a little weird. . . ."

Weird but necessary.

The writing knew—and I didn't—that on page 93 an intruder would crawl through a window and my heroine would need that gun.

I recently wrote a small novella, *Between Heaven and Earth*. The novella was in the form of letters between a husband and wife, separated by war. There were also letters from their children, twin boys.

Early on in the letters, a "bug project" showed up. Obediently, I wrote it down. Thinking, a "bug project"?

I did not realize that an entire image pattern was being set up. I did not know that the writing was planning to milk that bug project for all it was worth. I did not know that and I did not need to know that. I just needed to write "bug project" and then see what more was written on it later.

Many people—"nonwriters" if there is such a thing—think about writing a novel and imagine that in order to do it they must know everything before they start. No one could write a novel if that were the way it was done. And yet, unwittingly, "writers" can make it sound like they did know, did plan, did think their books through in advance. I think this comes from a certain understandable human tendency on the part of writers to puff themselves up a little to make themselves seem a little more brilliant. It is my experience that tremendous and subtle image patterns are discovered after we write them, not planned out before. To the reader this looks like careful construction, what the books call "foreshadowing." Maybe for some writers, a blessed few, it is a conscious act, but for the most part I think such claims to creative consciousness are hooey. I think we're just a little embarrassed to say, "Actually, that never consciously occurred to me . . ."

Regine now wants to write something longer than a poem—a screenplay—and the prospect has her terrified.

"How do you do it?" she wants to know. "You write books, movies, plays. They're all so long!"

"I'll tell you how I do it," I answer, "but that doesn't mean it is the way you should necessarily do it. There are as many ways to write as there are writers."

"Mmm." Clearly, Regine thinks I am waffling.

"One of my favorite writers, Ed, researches his novels carefully," I tell her. "He flies to where he's writing about, visits the town hall, the hall of records, the library, and the local interest spots. If he's going to write about a roadhouse, he goes to a roadhouse. If he's writing about horseracing, he goes to the track. He likes to saturate himself in atmosphere—then go home and write. That's his style."

"What's yours?"

"Oh, mine's very different."

"How?"

And so I began to tell Regine "how." More often than not, my stories, movies, and plays seem to choose me rather than vice versa. A voice starts talking in my head. If I agree to cooperate and listen to it, the voice unspools a story. The story contains vivid intimate details. I hear them as facts and write them down.

"Sort of like channeling?"

"I wouldn't use that word. I call it 'listening.'"

"What else?"

"Often I will begin to notice art, music, or collectibles from the area or era I am writing about. I will see a small smoked glass mirror and think, 'That's in my heroine's bedroom.' Or I will notice a small cut-glass perfume bottle and 'recognize' it from the dressing table in the boudoir. Sometimes a book will cross my path. When I delve into it, I will find it confirms the details I believed myself simply to have made up."

"That sounds a little eerie."

"Uncanny, maybe."

"So you don't research?"

"Not precisely. I focus on a certain situation, era, or locale and it's as if I am tuned into a radio band. I meet people who know all about cartography if I am writing about maps. I set out to describe Magellan's world and a young waiter brings me a copy of Magellan's clerk's diary. Out of the diary one detail will strike me—the clerk kept a secret stash of raisins which kept him from getting scurvy—and that detail will trigger a whole character, even a whole world."

"It sounds like blind luck."

"No. I believe we trigger this support. It's not luck. It's something closer to spiritual law."

"You really believe—"

"I really believe that we get help when we set out to write something. Yes. That is my experience."

"So you don't plan what you write?"

"I would say I dream it," I reply. "It's a sort of lucid dreaming where I carry the idea of the story and the Universe delivers to me bits and pieces as I need them."

"I can't dream a whole screenplay!" Regine retorts, disgusted by my somewhat ambiguous methods.

"My colleague John plans his movies," I tell her. "He writes outlines. Maybe you need to work like that. Or like my friend Mark, who plots his out scene by scene until it's almost like painting by numbers. Some writers rehearse their stories by telling them until they 'work.' I think that's dangerous because your writer may not know the difference between telling and telling it on the page. Too much telling makes my own writer feel stale when we actually get down to writing."

"You're not helping me," Regine complained. She said she kept seeing scenes and images, but she didn't know how they were spliced together.

"So write them out on index cards."

"Then what?"

"Break your story into three parts. Part one, you meet the characters and learn the questions of the film. Part two, you watch those questions play out through time. Part three, the questions are answered. Your scenes will fall into one of these three categories."

"They actually do."

"I know."

"So when do I start really writing?"

"That's up to you. You can keep building up cards until your story is very filled in or you can jump in early, like I do."

"Which works better?"

"It's which works better for you."

"Aaargh!"

Regine thinks I am holding out on her. I'm not. Writing is a personal process. We can pick up tips and hints from each other, but at its base, writing is a solitary act. We all do it alone and we all do it differently. As I said at the beginning, I write by sketching. I like to get down the general shape of something first and then go back and fill in later. I try not to censor. I put in what comes to me and I know that more will come later and that my first sketch will be a blueprint—and a prod—for finer and finer sketches, more and more detail.

"You make it sound so casual," Regine complains. "Like you just dash things off."

"I think dashing things off is a good thing," I answer. "We can dash off an awful lot of valid work relatively painlessly. When 'this is serious' sets in, so can writer's block."

"And does 'this is serious' always set in?"

"Almost always—yes, always."

My own experience is that somewhere around two thirds of the way through a piece I suddenly see what the writing was driving at. I see the patterns that have been set up and I get an idea where everything is heading. This point is a scary one. Now that "I" know what "I" am doing, I begin to worry that "I" might not be able to pull it off. In other words, my ego wakes up. No longer content to let the writing write through me, it suddenly demands control. It wants this book to be "good." This is the point that I call "The Wall." All writers know it.

The Wall is the point where a previously delightful project comes screeching to a halt. The Wall is the point where doubt sets in. No longer writing for the sake of writing, no longer happy just to splash in the pool, suddenly we think about those other people in the pool with us, whether they are faster, better, stronger, showier. In short, we begin to compete, not just create.

What can we do about this?

The first thing we usually try to do is pump ourselves up to power our way over the Wall: "This project's really great. I'm a really great writer. . . ."

I always picture convicts in an old forties movie trying to scale the wall—quick!—before the spotlight comes back around, freezing us in its glare as we slide—slowly—back to the ground under the guns drawn on our backs. No, trying to scale the Wall does not work.

So what does?

Again, go back to those old convict movies. How did they successfully escape? They burrowed under the wall. They crawled their way to freedom. This burrowing under the wall, this crawling, is what works to escape the prison of the ego.

So how do we crawl under the Wall?

Instead of "I'm great," we say, "I am willing to write badly. I am willing to do the work to finish this project whether it is any good or not."

When we insist on being great, the Wall stops us. When we are willing to be humble, we wriggle our way under the Wall and back to the glee of writing freely. By being willing to write "badly," we free ourselves to write—and perhaps to write very well. In other words, we go back to sketching.

I go back to that image of the apple tree. When I first sketched it in, it was a stick tree. Then I drew in little leaves. Then blossoms. Now it is a fragrant fluffy cloud. It's the same with writing. If we let ourselves sketch it in a little at a time, trusting each addition and doing only "the next right thing," our work blooms in the end.

SKETCHING
Initiation Tool

This tool is intended to help you find the joy and satisfaction that come from simply sketching. If "God is in the details," so is grace, and sketching is a means of contacting the grace-filled soup of where we really are.

Set aside one half hour. Settle yourself in to write. First take ten minutes to describe where you are and how you are. Sketch the room you are writing in, the mood you are writing in, anything delightful or interesting that catches your attention. Now number from one to five. Very quickly list five things it would be interesting to write about:

1. My grandparents
2. ESP
3. A ghost story
4. My daughter's dance recital
5. The Boer War

Choose one topic. What would you write about it? Why would you write about it? Spend five to ten minutes writing about that. Do not go for Art, capital "A," or even writing, capital "W." Think of this, instead, as word play. Do not worry about being deep or sensible or practical. Allow yourself to sketch this in the loosest, roughest terms.

LONELINESS

I HAVE SET A LARGE VASE of lilacs just to the left of me as I write. The flowers are heavy with scent. They are drowsy, aphrodisiac. They hold the same sway as a hammock on a hot summer afternoon.

I have put those flowers there to keep me company. Today I am lonely.

Our mythology tells us writers are loners. In fact, one of the most potent writer's blocks I know is the fear of loneliness that people associate with the writing life. Our mythology tells us that writers are loners and so, if you don't particularly want to be lonely, is it any wonder that you might postpone writing?

So much has been written about the loneliness of the writer's lot that it feels like heresy to report the truth as I know it: in my experience, *not* writing is a lonely business. The minute I let myself write, everything else falls into balance. If I get a dose of writing in my day, then I can actually socialize with a clear conscience. I can actually be present for the life I am having rather than living in the never-never land of the nonwriting writer, that twilight place where you always "should" be somewhere else—writing—so that you can never enjoy where you actually are.

I don't know why the mythology of writers as lone wolves is so pervasive and, for that matter, so persuasive. Some of our best writers were social animals. The youthful Hemingway had a far-flung net of friendships—Fitzgerald, Stein, Dos Passos—and a wide and passionate set of interests. Most writers are actually rather collegial, gathering in cafés, calling to grouse at one another on the phone. And yet, a great deal of fuss is always made about the loneliness of the writer's life. I believe it myself sometimes: "Poor me. I have to go into a room all alone and write. . . ."

But we do not go into a room all alone. We go into a room that is crowded by our own experiences, jammed to the rafters with our thoughts, feelings, friendships, gains, and losses. I am lonely today because I did not write enough yesterday. Not writing, I drop the thread of my consciousness. I lose track of myself. It is me, my consciousness, that I am missing. It is often disguised as missing someone else, and we do that too.

Today I am missing my friend David. He is in Europe, working, and I haven't heard from him. I miss the flow of his thoughts into my life. I miss his presence, the uncanny way he makes me laugh. David "gets" me. Part of what I am missing is the me that David gets. Writing this, I see that in not writing yesterday I lost sight of that me. I lost sight of her and I blamed it on David. I was actually missing us both.

My friend Laura called a moment ago. She called to talk about loneliness. At the moment she is separated for several months from her beloved.

"You know how I am getting through this," Laura tells me. "I am writing my way through it."

Not writing is the lonely thing. Not writing creates self-obsession. Self-obsession blocks connection with others. Self-obsession blocks connection with the self. Writing is like looking at an inner compass. We check in and we get our bearings. Ah-ha! I am feeling, thinking, remembering. . . . When we know accurately what it is that we are doing, we tend to be more open, accurate, and affectionate in our dealings: I can miss David, but I can't blame David anymore. I am the one who didn't write enough yesterday.

For this reason, I would argue that the writing life is a proof against loneliness. It is a balm for loneliness. It is an act of connection first to ourselves and then to others. Words are formed from "letters" and letters are what we are writing, really. Letters to ourselves. Letters to the world.

YOU

I am missing you.
My "I" stands like a lonely tree.
This landscape is denuded.

I am lying about that.
Lilacs are blooming.
Apple trees froth with lace.
Dandelions, daisies—
A full company is here.

All of them stand like a church
Without a steeple. It's incomplete.
You are my people.

Writing this little poem, I am able to name more accurately the fact that in addition to my writing—a loneliness I am mending—what I am missing is human companionship, conversation, ideas, talk. The poem tells me that after I finish writing, I will drive into the village and I will visit with shopkeepers, make the excuse of buying some nice paper to have a little talk. It is all a balancing act, all a question of proper ebb and flow.

***

Yesterday, the day I wasn't writing enough, I also did not go out. I stayed at home, fussing. I straightened papers, filed folders, "organized" myself. By evening I made a few phone calls, but my friends were busy and said they'd call me back. I settled in to watch a documentary, still hungry for a little chat. I had a sense that something wasn't right, wasn't finished.

When I don't write enough, I get a gnawing sense of disease. It is an appetite that isn't sated by other things. I become lonely for my soul. I try to find it by talking with people. I look for a glimpse of it at the movies. I clean my office to see where I misplaced it. I get lonely and pine and blame it on my friends. I try to set things right every way I know and then—after I have set up the vase of lilacs, cleaned the room, fussed at my thoughtless friends, I remember: oh, yes, I need to write. Maybe that's what's bothering me. . . .

I have a number of friends who are writers. It is easy for me to spot crankiness in them. It is easy for me to think, "Mmm. Ed's not writing enough. He's crabby" or, conversely, "Natalie must be writing a blue streak, she's so sunny these days."

"I can't talk now," John said when I called him two days ago. "For three weeks I've had houseguests and I am starved for some writing time. I just need to get to work. I've got to do some writing."

I recognize the urgency in John's need to write. Over the long term, writing is a lot like marathon running and, just as a runner suffers withdrawal when unable to run for a day or two, so, too, does a working writer miss his writing work. A certain amount of writing, like a certain amount of miles, keeps the artistic athlete happy and fit. Without this regular regime, tensions build up. Irritability sets in. Life becomes somehow far less hospitable. A good writing day rights this again.

I have many friends who are not writers, and writing helps them too. As a sort of creative nurse-practitioner, I have sometimes suggested to despairing friends that they give themselves the gift of three longhand pages every morning to see if it doesn't cheer them up. It cheers them up. It energizes them. It gives them a sense of flow.

Writing runs through my life like a river. There is always the sound of it, sometimes louder than others, as when the Rio Grande, my neighboring river, is made loud and raucous with the floods of melting springtime snow. Other times it is quieter, a sort of *plash, plash, plash*. Sometimes it is so quiet, I need to move closer to hear the flow, but the flow is always there, always a companion. It is like the sound of surf, so constant and repetitive, it becomes white noise, a sound that isn't missed until you move too far inland and lose it.

"Losing it," the flow of writing, is what makes for loneliness. It's also a matter of faith. When I am not writing, when I am not "right-

' myself, I slip into a gentle and sometimes not so gentle form of paranoia. I feel dislocated. Out of synch. Out of sorts and out of step. This sense of disconnection from the family of man is a symptom of not writing enough. When I am writing often enough, I find myself interested by what I am saying. Interested myself, it is easier for me to believe that others might be interested. Conversely, as I empty myself onto the page, there is more room for other people's thoughts, other people's ideas. There is, in short, more room for companionship. Less room for loneliness.

LONELINESS
Initiation Tool

This tool is intended to give you a higher perspective. So often our loneliness comes because we have lost the overview, the sense of the large sweep and movement in our lives. In this tool you are asked to try directly contacting what may feel to you like a mythological or archetypal character, Older Self. For some of us, this character feels a little like Obi-Wan Kenobi from *Star Wars,* for others it is Merlin, the Lady of the Lake, or even a benevolent fairy godmother. At base, this Older Self, however you conceptualize it—and it may surprise you as it speaks—is essentially a spiritual companion.

Set aside one hour. If you're writing at home, make yourself a cup of tea, cocoa, or coffee. If you're writing "out," enjoy a mulled cider, cappuccino, smoothie, or anything else soothing. Get comfortable, put your hand to the page, and allow an older and wiser eighty-year-old you to write you a letter about your life. Allow your Older Self to give you a sense of perspective, guidance, and right action. Write for one half hour, longer if you choose. This is a writing tool you may wish to use regularly.

WITNESS

THIS MORNING I got a phone call from a friend of mine who is in hard times. Her voice was high, agitated, unstrung. She talked rapidly, in great loping circles. I could hear her pacing as she talked. Several times she stopped to light a cigarette. Even on the long distance wire, when she inhaled, it was like she was sucking on an air hose. She was panicked, "undone," grieving over multiple repetitive losses with no place to grieve them in a modern world. Her therapist was on vacation in a foreign country. Her family was out of touch.

"Am I bothering you?" she wanted to know. "I must sound crazy."

I told her, no, she didn't sound crazy. She sounded sad and frantic with grief.

"I guess I do," she said. "So many things have happened." She ticked them off: the death of a beloved pet, the injury of another, the anniversary of a parent's death, another close friend, ailing . . .

After we talked for about an hour, I said, "Maybe you might want to try writing."

I got off the phone and thought about what I had said and done. What did I think my friend needed that writing could offer?

I think my friend needs a witness. I think we all do.

So much of the loneliness of modern life comes because we no longer witness each other. Our lives are led at such velocity that we often feel—and are—quite alone. My friends are scattered. My family is scattered. I am in Taos, New Mexico, but those closest to me are in Dublin, Connecticut, New York, Boston, London, Bath, Brasilia. We stay in touch by phone and fax, but it is iffy.

Tonight, writer Sonia Choquette is giving a reading in Denver. I phoned the bookstore to say, "Have a great evening. I'll talk to you afterward." The bookstore wasn't sure they could get the message to her. Last week I faxed David in London and the fax went to someone else entirely. David walked into a meeting and someone said, "I've got your fax from Julia Cameron. . . ." Evers to Tinker to Chance, and Chance can be a tricky catch.

Even with the best intentions, even with the most modern technology, it is sometimes hit or miss—or Mercury retrograde, those three periods a year when astrologers will tell you that communications go kablooey. We need more and better witness, closer and more personal tenderness than we can offer each other long distance despite our good intentions.

I told my friend, "If you were in a little village in India, going through this grief, this series of griefs, people would not expect you to 'function.' They would expect you to grieve. Our modern ideas of 'functioning' through things are really quite inhuman. We have this idea that no matter what is going on we still have to color between the lines, act normal. Do we?"

"I think we do," my friend said cautiously. "I certainly feel like I owe it to people to act OK so they won't worry."

"There has to be someplace where we can fall apart."

"Yes, yes, there does." My friend sounded relieved at the thought.

"For me, that place is writing."

I heard a pause while my friend was thinking—trying to think—through her swirling thinking.

She finally spoke. "Actually, I have been writing. I've just started to. Yesterday I wrote my husband this long five-page letter."

"That's what I'm talking about," I told her. "I started writing Morning Pages when I was going through a divorce. I needed a place to place my grief."

"And that's when you started the writing in the morning? That's what it's for?"

"That's one of the things that it's for."

"Maybe I should actually try those Morning Pages," my friend said. "I've always thought of them as, oh, Julia's thing, but maybe they could work for me."

"Maybe they could."

What writing brings to a life is clarity and tenderness. Writing, we witness ourselves. We say, like our own village elders, "I knew you when you were knee high and you've certainly come a long way."

Writing gives us a place to say, "I miss my dog Ripley. He was so merry and kissy. He was such a buoyant, bonnie little dog." Writing gives us a place to say, "It is two years this week since Dad died. Maybe I should buy some birdhouses like he always did." Writing gives us a place to say what we need to say, but also to hear what we need to hear.

My Morning Pages might equally well be called "Mentoring Pages" because they help me to access a warmer and wiser part of myself than my busy modern business persona. Although I grouse and complain on the page, I also marvel and appreciate. I am my own village gossip: "Did you see that? Did you hear what she said?" Writing also suggests, "Maybe she meant . . ." It makes me compassionate.

Christine is a woman in a committed but often difficult marriage. Her husband, orphaned as a child, periodically retreats into a shell when he feels threatened or off center. No amount of warmth and coaxing can lure him back out until time and distance have eased whatever wounded him. For Christine, her husband's withdrawals are painful and they can create intense feelings of abandonment and betrayal. She uses her writing to keep her in touch with her own heart and needs and connected, too, to the part of her that can understand and weather her husband's emotional storms.

"My pages will urge me to go for a walk, buy some nice yarn for knitting, water-color place settings for my niece's graduation party," Christine tells me. "My pages will tell me that my husband is only hurt and frightened, not leaving me, and that even if my own husband can't see it at the moment, I am a warm and loving woman. My pages will urge, 'make soup' or 'bake pies.' They will tell me to buy pretty stamps or to remember to burn incense. In a thousand little ways the writing keeps me from abandoning myself. I often feel that my writing is like a wise best friend who cherishes me and has only my best interests at heart."

In other words, Christine's writing bears witness. Bearing witness is a more active process than we may at first perceive. My horse Bob Hope has tiny little ears that twitch forward with curiosity, staring over the pasture fence and through the study window when he notices me up to something. His perked ears make me stop a moment and think, "What am I doing that's unusual here?" Writing-as-witness helps me ask the same question.

Joseph is an executive who uses writing to help him stay connected to himself throughout his long and hectic business days.

"I just have so much to metabolize," Joseph phrases it. "In any given day I meet so many people and do so many things that I need a place to ask myself what I really think about all of it. Without writing, my life rushes by unexamined and I feel a disturbing sense of disconnection. When I write, I seem to be able to touch base with myself so there's some sense of Joseph the person rather than just Joseph the functionary."

Writing notices the shifts of direction, the subtle darkening of a mood or relationship. Conversely, writing points out the good things: a new and sunny friendship crammed with jokes, high jinks, and high spirits. "This is a switch," the writing says. "This is really groovy."

"We don't stop," David writes me of his work life in London, where he is in meetings morning until midnight. He underlines, "stop," stopping long enough to write me.

Our modern lives are vertical with exertion. They are fraught, demanding, difficult. We need someone, someplace, to hear how hard they are. We need, and we must learn to be, our witness.

WITNESS
Initiation Tool

The tool I ask you to undertake now is the most profound writer's tool I have devised or experienced. Called "Morning Pages," this tool is the bedrock of a writing life. Morning Pages bear witness to our lives. They increase our conscious contact with spiritual guidance.

They prioritize our days while they miniaturize our censor, allowing us to write more freely and effectively. So what, exactly, are they?

Mornings Pages are three pages of daily longhand writing, strictly stream of consciousness. They are about anything and everything that crosses your mind. They may be petty, whiny, boring, angry. They may be cheerful, illuminating, insightful, and introspective. There is no wrong way to do them. You simply move your hand across the page while writing down whatever comes to mind: "Dad's cough is getting worse . . . I forgot to buy Kitty Litter . . . I don't like how things went in yesterday's meeting . . ."

Yes, Morning Pages are done in the morning. Most people find they take somewhere between twenty-five and forty-five minutes. "Julia, I don't have time!" many of my students have exclaimed. I ask them—and you—to try them anyway. Set your clock a half hour early and just do them using 8½ by 11 pages. (Smaller pages tend to crimp our thoughts; larger pages take us too far too fast and simply take too long.)

Yes, Morning Pages must be done in the morning. They prioritize the day we are about to have. (If we do them in the evening, we are reviewing the day we've already had—and are powerless to change.) At root, Morning Pages are profoundly helpful. They calm us down. They cheer us up. They console us. They inspire us. Morning Pages are for Westerners a uniquely potent form of meditation. They allow us to empty our minds and hearts of disturbing distractions and simultaneously open our minds and hearts to deeper reflections.

It's important the pages be done longhand. There is an energy to the hand that leads our thoughts to a deeper and more connected place than writing on the keys does. True, computers are faster, but fast is not always better even if our culture says that it is. So do your pages by hand if at all possible and do them first thing in the morning.

You want to catch your mind before it has its defenses up. You want to surprise it when it's still close to your dreaming consciousness. You do not want your Morning Pages to march like perfect little soldiers, to be a carefully manufactured product of your rational workaday self. What you do want is to catch yourself unawares, to record things you didn't really know you were thinking. So simply move your hand across the page, recording whatever comes to mind. Do this daily for three pages.

"Morning Pages changed my life," students often tell me. I know this to be true in my own life and I know it to be true in the lives of those I've taught. Whether it was a room full of college students at Northwestern University, where I served as writer in residence, or a room full of fifty-year-olds at a creativity camp in Connecticut, I have seen Morning Pages quite literally "turn on the lights" in people's faces. In California I've heard jokes that Morning Pages are an alternative to face-lifts and that people should do them for vanity alone. Truth be told, they do make you feel better, and people who feel better often do show it. So try them.

Try Morning Pages from here on out as you work with this book. A substantial shift in consciousness can be felt within ninety days (the length of time the brain needs to "groove" a new neurological pattern), but often a shift is felt much sooner. Be alert to your own process and progress with pages. Be your own self-validating witness.

Why Don't We Do
It in the Road?

I'd love to be a writer, but I just don't have the discipline," people tell me. I know what they mean: neither do I.

I am someone who has been writing "full-time" now for thirty years. If I had to do it the way that people think it is done—with "discipline"—I am not sure that I would be able to do it at all.

Right now I am working with a fitness trainer. I hate going to the gym. I hate every stitch of what I am doing with her, but I just show up and grouse through it. "Someday you will love this," my trainer says to me. "Someday you won't be able to wait to work out."

Not likely, I think.

Talking about writing and the idea that "someday you will love it and look forward to it," I feel like I am about as convincing as my trainer. But the truth is that I do love it and that I do not find it a discipline. I do not put in long hours at the keys—or very seldom. Instead, I snatch time. I write in the crannies of my life. I make my writing desk the most enticing corner—and sometimes corners—of my house. My desk has toys. My desk has flowers. My desk has pictures of my beloved daughter, Domenica, as a baby, and I do baby myself as I write.

People who write out of "discipline" are taking a substantial risk. They are setting up a situation against which they may one day strongly rebel. Writing from discipline invites extremism: "I have to do this or I'm a failure." Writing from discipline creates a potential for emotional blackmail: "If I don't write I've got no character."

People who write from discipline also take the risk of trying to write from the least open and imaginative part of themselves, the part of them that punches a time clock instead of taking flights of fancy. "Commitment" is a word I prefer to the word "discipline." It is more proactive, more heart-centered, and ultimately more festive and productive. This is not mere semantics. If we are to be involved with writing for the long haul, we want to be comfortable in relationship to it. If we are relating to our writing as a "should" instead of as a desired good, we run the jeopardy of experiencing our writing connection like a thankless marriage: we're there, but we don't want to be. We're thinking of what we're missing.

This morning I woke up at 5:45 just as the sun was clearing the mountains—"A little early," I thought, but I felt rested.

I went out to the kitchen, put on a pot of coffee, and settled in on the couch amid a cache of new videos to write my Morning Pages. By now I am quite fast at them, and so in twenty minutes I was done and thinking about what I wanted to do. I'd had about twenty seconds to think before a song suggested itself, so I wrote it out and then sang it into a tape recorder. By the time I was ready to start notating it, the phone rang and it was Domenica from Ireland. She is finding her sea legs as a writer.

"I spent my morning writing out Blasting through Blocks," she said, referring to a writing exercise that functions as a jump start on creative projects. "You want to hear my fears and resentments and what I'd really like to write?"

"Sure."

Domenica then read off a list of her "stuff," which sounded remarkably like my own "stuff"—and like everyone's—before heading into a piece of work.

"I'm afraid I'm lousy."

"I'm afraid I'm good but no one will think so."

"I'm afraid this work won't work."

"I'm afraid this work will work but no one will see that."

"I'm afraid I'm stupid."

"I'm afraid . . ."

"How do you feel now?" I asked Domenica after she'd shared her list.

"Better. Less afraid. More like I'd actually like to write."

"Oh, good."

"I'm afraid" is always what stands between us and the page. When people talk about "discipline," they are really talking about "how do you get past 'I'm afraid.'"

The fears may not be conscious, and that's what makes it tricky. When we are procrastinating about writing something or someone, we are always being backed off by our fears. It may be disguised as our business or our "need to focus" or any number of other distractions, but it boils down to our fear of revealing ourselves to others and ourselves.

Coming out of the work ethic, when we think about writing we think about being marched at gunpoint to the page. This leftover Calvinism so endemic to the American character is why we think that writing takes discipline. We think we have to be "ready" to write. We think there's no place for showing up dressed come-as-you-are. We think of writing as a state occasion. We think of writing as a commitment. We think of writing as a great many things except for its dominant nature: fun.

Yes, fun. There are other words we could use: "satisfying," "fulfilling," "gratifying," but those are very adult words for what is on many levels a very instinctual experience. We "think" of writing as being cerebral, but when we actually engage in it, it is far more grounded and gut level than that.

On a very primal level, writing is naughty. It is an act of self-possession. "This is what I think . . ." There is an anarchistic two-year-old inside most of us, and that child likes to have its say. When we let writing be about that, when we think of it as sharing secrets with ourselves, gleeful at what we are daring to do, writing doesn't take much "discipline."

Right now I have a window onto a new friend's world. That world is rock and roll: flashing lights, booming bass, sweat and strobe lights. I watch that world on my stash of videos, and I don't hear the songbirds outside my window until everyone bobs their heads a final time and runs from the stage.

The videos are of music caught "live." That's what writing is like. We think of it as something classical, something for which we must be schooled and polished, but it can be live, sweat and all. It can be learning a few chords on a beat-up guitar. It can be the voice cracking and the cockeyed grin right in the middle of a solo. Writing doesn't have to be prettied up. Writing doesn't have to be perfect. Writing is about energy, about perfect imperfection, about humanity.

When writing gets to be a work in progress, when writing gets to be real "live" rock and roll, then writing becomes infectious instead of disciplined. Writing becomes "Just do it" and "Hey, let's dance."

When it comes to writing, too many of us are like wallflowers at the party. We make a big deal out of getting out on the floor. We want to do it "right" when what we really want is just to do it. Like sex: going without writing can certainly be done, can even get to be a comfortable habit, but going with it can get to be a habit too. Like sex, writing is a human drive. The drive to name things, to speak, is perhaps our third instinctual drive: "Feed me, touch me, let me tell you how it feels."

One of my favorite pieces of rock and roll is the rock opera *Tommy* with its refrain "See me, touch me, feel me, heal me." That is what writing is all about. It is that basic, that primal, that rock and roll.

"But, Julia, I'm not that hip."

None of us is that hip and all of us are.

One of the best jazz piano players I know is a nun. Rosario Carelli, who teaches West African drumming, tells me that everybody can play, everybody has rhythm, everybody can speak "drum" and hear "drum." Communicating is a natural human drive. We all speak the mother tongue and we do it a number of ways.

"Why don't we do it in the road?" the Beatles asked.

That's how we can do writing.

Writing is about making brain children. When it comes to conception, it can but doesn't need to be missionary position.

Don't make it so fancy. Do it on the kitchen table. Let your prose flash like Jessica Lange's white panties in *The Postman Always Rings Twice*. Do it in a back pew at church. Do it outside next to the lilac bush. Do it in the bathtub. Do it in a café. On an airplane. Do it, do it, do it.

When I first became well known as a creativity teacher, people would ask me how it felt. "Like Masters and Johnson," I would tell them. "It's fun to help people do something that feels good, but it's even more fun to do it myself."

This essay might strike some people as unduly libidinous. We *are* libidinous. We *are* writers.

"Take off your clothes . . ."

"Take off your prose . . ."

"Slip into something more comfortable. . ."

Writing is something more comfortable than not writing. Writing is something more fun. Something more comfortable and more fun does not take "discipline." It takes permission, self-permission. I don't write to be hard on myself. I write to be easy on myself. I write because it feels good.

"Yeah, but you're a writer. You do it well. That's why it feels good."

I said it was like sex, didn't I? It feels good whether you do it well or not. It feels bad only when we've got performance anxiety, when we're doing it and thinking "How am I doing it?"

When it comes to writing, we are trained to self-consciousness, trained to performance anxiety. We can untrain ourselves. We can do it in the road. We can all, naturally, do it. Writing is in the genes. Or, since this essay has more than a little rock and roll in it, "It's in the jeans."

In other words, it's in what's comfortable, wearable, easy.

"But, Julia, I never wear blue jeans. I'm more formal than that."

OK. So set a formal writing time. Meet yourself like a dinner date. Whatever fits is the key. Whatever feels easy.

I wear my writing like an old pair of Chinese silk pajamas. I like it loose and easy. My friend Alex suits up to write. He likes it structured. He goes to an office.

What matters is that each of us must find our own writing style. Some of us are morning writers. Some of us write late at night. Some of us watch the clock. Some of us count pages. Some of us write in cafés. Others of us need quiet libraries. With luck and a little practice, you can have several writing styles depending on how you feel. The point is to get comfortable. The point is to be formal only insofar as it serves you.

It doesn't matter how you do it, what matters is that you do it.

In *Pulp Fiction,* the girlfriend wonders why having a little tummy can feel so good to the owner and get such a bad rap the rest of the time. I know just what she means. When it comes to writing, it's OK to have a little tummy. It's OK to write sentences with curves. It doesn't have to be flat, hard, chiseled prose, the washboard prose they teach us in school. Writing as sit-ups. That's what we learn. Writing can be more comfortable than that. Writing can be earthy.

WHY DON'T WE DO IT
IN THE ROAD?
Initiation Tool

By now your writing is becoming portable. This tool asks you to take it on the road. Set aside one hour's time. Select a place where you can go and observe life in action: a coffee shop, a concert, a dentist's office, a shopping mall. Go somewhere active and go there notepad in hand. Set your hand to the page and start describing what you see and how you feel about what you see. Let yourself comment fully on the lady in the funny hat, the grumpy man with the fat cigar, the crying baby, the smitten lovers. Write rapidly and accurately. Describe the scene unfolding around you. Toy shops are an excellent place to visit. So are bridal shops. Allow yourself to be a real reporter. Record what your eyes see and your ears hear.

Remember gonzo journalist Hunter Thompson's advice that the secret of good writing lies in good notes. What's on the walls? What kind of windows are there? Who's talking? What are they saying? Write for one hour, then stop. You may find yourself wishing to post this exercise as a letter.

CONNECTION

O<small>URS IS A</small> perishable age. We have cup of soup meals and entire relationships. We talk on the phone. We say, "I love you. I miss you," but, as the truism correctly has it, actions speak louder than words and the act of putting it in writing says as much, and more, than the words themselves. Writing is old-fashioned, but it helps us to survive and connect in a modern world.

This morning I received a one-page fax from Europe. It was handwritten, block letters, a note really. No big deal, but I loved getting it. It was real as salt.

"Put it in writing," we say when we are talking about contracts. Our human contacts are contracts too, but we seldom put them in writing anymore, and when we do, the shift it creates can be astonishing.

"Never put anything in writing," a mafioso once told me—hilarious advice to a writer but good advice for a thug who didn't want to get caught in his thuggishness.

I would say, "Do put it in writing."

"It" being whatever "it" is.

"Let me write it down for you," we say about recipes, and writing "it" down can be a recipe for a far tastier, far more savory life.

Recipes are precise, even if their language is offhand, "A pinch of salt." Writing out how we feel and what we think is also precise—

even if what we are writing is "I'm not sure about what's going on between us right now."

Writing is a way not only to metabolize life but to alchemize it as well. It is a way to transform what happens to us into our own experience. It is a way to move from passive to active. We may still be the victims of circumstance, but by our understanding those circumstances we place events within the ongoing context of our own life, that is, the life we "own."

Owning something also means owning up to something. It means accepting responsibility, which means, literally, response-ability. When we write about our lives we respond to them. As we respond to them we are rendered more fluid, more centered, more agile on our own behalf. We are rendered conscious. Each day, each life, is a series of choices, and as we use the lens of writing to view our lives, we see our choices.

For four years I was in a working relationship with a man who was distant and often difficult. In my head I could rationalize his aloofness as a by-product of his upbringing, as the natural manifestation of his astrological chart, as any number of things. That was in my head.

On the page I wrote, "This doesn't feel good, this constant hide-and-seek. It's tiresome and it deflects my creative energies. I am not sure I can or should afford this."

Then I wrote, "He reminds me of my horse Walter. For twelve years I have fed Walter, and whenever I go to pat him he sticks his muzzle in the air, declaring: I am Walter. I am special. I am a beautiful snow-white Arabian. You may admire me but never catch me. I am elusive. I am special. I am Walter. . . ."

Writing out this insight, I felt something large shifting inside me. "This is a game I do not want to play," I wrote on. "The inevitable dynamic here is about power—power manifested and maintained through withholding. This will never be a satisfying and easy relationship. I think I'll quit. . . ."

And I quit.

Without my writing, I would not have seen this dynamic. If this sounds as if I am saying writing is therapy, let me be clear that I feel writing is something therapy often is not: writing is therapeutic.

Writing connects the self to the Self.

For nearly two decades, I have been working with students and watching those students transform their lives through writing. I have seen shy and timorous students claim their right. I have seen bombastic, blowhard students gently deflate their own egos and become user-friendly members of the human tribe. I have watched people open themselves to deeper relationships, extricate themselves from difficult relationships, change jobs, and change identities. I have seen writing work less like a tool than a medicine. It is a medicine all of us can make and administer to ourselves.

This book is called *The Right to Write,* and if that sounds like a manifesto, or a call to arms, it is because my own experience has taught me that my "right to write" is what gives me the many other rights I now insist on: respect for my work, respect for me as a person, relationships involving give as well as take.

Robert began writing six months ago. As he undertook writing, he was deeply enmeshed in a relationship that managed to marginalize him in his own life. His girlfriend—if that is an accurate word for someone who perceived herself as his warden and keeper—had many opinions and judgments that she freely extended to all areas of Robert's life—his creative work, his friendships, his business alliances—all of them passed under her scrutiny, and nothing ever cut the mustard. There was always some fault, some flaw, some fatal lack that Robert "should" have seen and would have if he weren't himself so somehow flawed, somehow shortsighted, somehow, well, lacking.

Robert began confiding his life to the page. He found quickly that he loved having a forum to air his own thoughts, process his own life, examine his own opinions. Within a month the dynamic of Robert and his girlfriend began shifting. He began withholding information that she would use against him. He began drawing lines around the areas where her opinions were not welcome. By the second month Robert was no longer available for emotional blackmail. He began drawing boundaries. Her assaults on his character met with new resistance and resiliency.

For three months after that Robert journaled his feelings about possibly ending the relationship, which he had previously seen as permanent, his "fate." Six months into writing Robert wrote his girlfriend a letter formally severing their relationship. Then Robert, milksop, browbeaten Robert, took off for a three-month trip to India. His letters indicate he is having a wonderful time.

For me, like Robert, writing has been the way I have done my cartography. Writing has allowed me to map my miseries and my delights, my boundaries and my greater plains of generosity. Writing has allowed me to say, "This is where I must stop and you must begin." Writing has allowed me to say, "Yes, we are in 'this' together."

Writing tells us that we are not powerless. Writing tells us that we have choices. Writing tells us what those choices are. Writing tells us when we are shirking responsibility. Writing tells us when we are overburdened. Writing tells us when we love the status quo—"This is a great happiness/ The air is like silk/ There is milk in the looks that come from strangers . . ."—and when we want a change. Writing, we effect that change.

"The way we describe our lives and understand them is ultimately and inextricably connected to the way we live them," writes therapist and writing coach Mandy Aftel. She adds, "In a very real sense, we are the authors of our own lives."

If we are the "authors" of our own lives, why not rewrite them more actively? Why not make those lives more romantic, more personally satisfying? Why not write love letters to our beloveds? Why not tell them on the page: "You, I cherish"?

Right now I have a new friendship that is literally unfolding a page at a time. Across countries and continents, across time zones and buffeted by jet lag, two of us are chirping communiqués, field reports on our far-flung and modern lives.

I am reminded of what the Aboriginals called "songlines." These were the trails the ancestors walked, crisscrossing the continent down under, mapping it and naming it in song, a step at a time. My friend and I, walking continents apart, are singing songlines. "This was my day in Paris . . . This was mine in the Sangre de Cristo mountains."

If we will use writing to connect to ourselves, I believe we can connect across time and space and distance. I believe in the global village we are making, and I believe that in order to make that village truly habitable, we will need to return to the page. We use the expression "I am paging him" when we speak of trying to get someone's attention at some busy intersection—a convention, an international airport, a large manufacturing concern. Our world, our global village, is all of these things, and if we want to get one another's attention, we do need to "page," in the slightly different sense that we need to write.

"The dessert was—I can't on short notice come up with a superlative to describe it. How about 'amazing' or 'unbelievable'"? This compliment came to me by mail after I'd made a meal for a fellow writer that included strawberry pie with homemade whipped cream. The note, a few minutes in the making, made the meal, a few hours in the making, seem even more enjoyable in the savoring afterward.

So much of what we need, so much of what we want, is to be savored, cherished, cared for, and cared about. So much of what is missing is tenderness. When we commit our thoughts to paper, we send a strong and clear message that what we are writing about and whom we are writing to matters. As Sonia Choquette, spiritual teacher, advises us, "The power of the word is real whether or not you are conscious of it. Your own words are the bricks and mortar of the dreams you want to realize. Behind every word flows energy."

I would add, not only "behind" every word, but "through" every word. It is my belief that writing is one of the most powerful ways available to us to not only "right" ourselves but also right the world. As I write this book, I am sending snatches of it off to David. He writes, "It is especially good to get the essays."

"It is good that I am able to be a work in progress with you," I write back.

We are all works in progress. We are all rough drafts. None of us is finished, final, "done." How much healthier and happier if we ignore that mafioso's advice to me and we put "it"—all of "it"—in writing: the flaws, foibles, frills, fantasies, and frailties that make us human.

When we connect these dots, we connect.

CONNECTION
Initiation Tool

This is another tool of spiritual companionship, a tool that affords us a deeper sense of personal connection to the journey of our own life. For this tool, you will one more time need to set aside a quiet hour, this time in a gentle private space. You may want to light a candle and cue up some soothing music like Michael Hoppe's album *The Yearning*. You are going to use this hour to connect to a younger you, someone you might think of as Younger Self. Just as you did with your eighty-year-old Older Self, you are going to give this Younger Self the chance to speak to you directly through a personal letter. So set your hand to the page, drop down the well, and let your Younger Self speak to you of its wishes, hopes, thoughts, concerns, and dreams. Do not censor anything your inner youngster has to tell you. Sometimes these letters can provoke strong emotions. Be prepared for that and keep your hand moving across the page.

Write for at least a half hour. Take a few deep breaths, then read and absorb what your inner youngster had to say. Your connection to this part of yourself is an important part of your writing life. It's good that we are getting acquainted.

Being an Open Channel

Much ado is frequently made about writers and their rituals. Writing, so the stories go, takes total concentration, a mustering of all intellectual energies—that and more. Special pens. Special notebooks. The desk clear and in perfect order. The phones off. The family backed off or somehow corralled. Privacy, even sanctity, is demanded. The writing space becomes a sanctum sanctorum. . . .

I don't like to make such a big deal out of writing.

I like writing to be more portable and flexible. I like writing to be something that fits into cracks and crannies. I don't like it to dominate my life. I like it to fill my life. There is a big difference. When writing dominates a life, relationships suffer—and, not coincidentally, so does the writing. When writing is about being shut off from the world in a room sequestered with our own important thoughts, we lose the flow of life, the flow of new ideas and input that can shape, improve, and inform that thought. It is a matter of balance. Yes, we need time and space to write, but we do not perhaps need as much time and as much space as we might think. Rather than being a private affair cordoned off from life as the rest of the world lives it, writing might profitably be seen as an activity best embedded in life, not divorced from it—of course such a view of writing smacks of heresy.

The phone just rang and on the line was my friend Martha Hamilton Snyder, a homeopath and channel. We talked about the place of "interruptions" in our life. We both tend to view interruptions as interventions, even corrections, in our trajectory.

"I can be doing a reading for someone," Martha said, "have my dogs stage a fit and need some attention, say, 'Just a minute. I'll be right back,' then deal with my dogs and come right back just fine."

In fact, from my years of talking with Martha, I have often noticed she comes back with something more than "just fine." She comes back with a fresh thought or insight gained in the moment she was "interrupted" in her work. The same saving dynamic seems to work in my own work.

This morning Martha's "interruption" functioned for me as a correction: I was writing about the need to be casual in our writing, but I wasn't talking about how to do that. Listening to Martha, I thought, "Ah. That's the piece I wasn't saying: 'channeling.'"

When writing is perceived as channeling spiritual information rather than inventing intellectual information, writing becomes a more fluid process that we are no longer charged with self-consciously guarding. Instead, we are charged with being available to it. We can "plug in" to the flow of writing rather than thinking of it as a stream of energy we must generate from within ourself.

Our ego wants to say, "I am writing and I cannot be interrupted and pulled away from *my* thoughts." The actual artistic reality, the experience of artists throughout time, is something far different and far more humble. As artists, we make ourselves available for thoughts to come through us. To the degree that we can set ego aside, we can create freely. We tune in to a stream of inspiration. We allow it to flow through us. We are an "open channel."

"Channeling? Julia, that word is so . . ."

I know. I know and I do not care, because the word is artistically accurate. Many people have an aversion to channeling as a word and as a concept. It seems too "New Age" or too nebulous and airy-fairy. And yet, it is essentially a way of talking about the creative process that has been reiterated over and over by artists throughout the centuries. Listen a second:

"The music of this opera *(Madame Butterfly)* was dictated to me by God. I was merely instrumental in getting it on paper and communicating it to the public."—Giacomo Puccini

"Straightaway the ideas flow in upon me, directly from God."—
Johannes Brahms

"The position of the artist is humble. He is essentially a channel."—Piet Mondrian

"I myself do nothing. The Holy Spirit Himself accomplishes all through me."—William Blake

It could be argued that the artists I am quoting come from earlier times, times when it was acceptable to attribute inspiration to "God." I think acceptability has less to do with it than accuracy; these men are simply reporting their own experience. My contemporaries in the arts report much the same thing.

"I don't play my music. It's not my music. It's God's music. It's God or the Great Spirit playing through me," says Robert Jackson, an exquisite flute player. "Once I realized it wasn't 'my' music, once I realized I was essentially a straw, I began to play very beautiful music—but it is not 'mine.' It's God's."

Although we seldom talk about it in these terms, writing is a means of prayer. It connects us to the invisible world. It gives us a gate or a conduit for the other world to talk to us whether we call it the subconscious, the unconscious, the superconscious, the imagination, or the Muse. Writing gives us a place to welcome more than the rational. It opens the door to inspiration. It opens the door to God or, if you would, to "Good Orderly Direction." Writing is a spiritual housekeeper. Writing sets things straight, giving us a sense of our true priorities.

No matter how secular it may appear, writing is actually a spiritual tool. We undertake it solo, and, not to be too facile with puns, it is worth noting that that word does have the word "soul" embedded in it. Moving alone onto the page, we often find ourselves companioned by higher forces, by a stream of insights and inspirations that seem somehow "other" than our routine thinking.

Artists throughout the centuries have noticed this higher dimension and called it "God." It doesn't matter what you call it. The point is that writing allows you to contact it. Whether you think of it as

"God" or "higher forces," as "inspiration" or as contact with your own "higher self" doesn't really matter. What does matter is that you can access a source of information and guidance, both creative and mundane, that will serve you.

Viewed this way—as a form of contact with something larger than ourselves—writing does not remain an ego-centered activity we are doing by our brilliant selves. It does not remain something that must be protected from life. It becomes, instead, a part of life, a co-operative pas de deux rather than a star turn.

The temptation to make our writing "mine," particularly when it's going well, is an understandable human impulse. It is, in a sense, the impulse to hoard. Rather than stay in the process of creating, we get attached to some particular creation. We think, "Wow. This is a real jewel, and I made it."

"This is the best piece of writing I have done in twenty years. I am really proud of it," I recently wrote David about a novella. As I wrote the words, a little internal buzzer sounded: Watch out . . . It's all very well for me to think the work is good. It *is* good but whether it is "mine" is a very different question. I know that if I tell the truth about what I experienced, I did have the experience of receiving this work, not creating it. I was the listener, not the speaker. I was, as Piet Mondrian put it, in the position of being "essentially a channel."

I wrote a series of letters between a husband and a wife separated by war. I say, "I wrote," but that is not really my experience of what happened. My experience is that I was chosen as a channel to view and write down a very real relationship between two people who were fully formed without my having to do anything in the way of invention. They had their own voices, opinions, pasts. I saw their house, met their children. I knew what the bathrooms and bedrooms looked like, what the driveway was like, what the backyard looked like. I "knew." I did not invent. I did not "make up." I simply wrote down what was shown to me. When the piece was finished, my ego kicked in.

The ego hates being a "channel"—or whatever other nonoffensive word you can find for it. The ego wants to take credit—but the ego never wants to take "blame." The ego wants to have it both ways:

to receive the work effortlessly and then take the full glory for having "thought it all up" instead of "taking it all down."

It is possible to write out of the ego. It is possible, but it is also painful and exhausting. Back in my drinking days, I used to strain to be brilliant, to write the best, the most amazing, most dazzling. . . . Is it any wonder that chemical additives seemed like a good idea, like the secret hidden advantage I just might need?

Once I stopped drinking, I found all attempts to be a "great" writer or even a "good" writer to be both exhausting and somehow beside the point. I began to sense that writing was about something larger than "career." I began to sense that writing was about writing itself. What I needed to do was simply write and not worry so much about judging it. But how?

I was told by screenwriters Jerry Ayres and Diana Gould, and by nonfiction writer Maurice Zolotow, to post a little sign by my desk that said something like, "OK, Universe. You take care of the quality. I'll take care of the quantity."

Good advice, all, but my ego bridled at this new humility, wondering if this meant I had "no standards." As I told them, I "had my reservations." Nonetheless, I tried their advice and my writing freed up immediately. Some days the writing seemed good to me. Other days it seemed less good. But I was writing regularly and with relative ease.

I came to the humbling conclusion that over time I wrote pretty much the same level all the time, a few peaks and a few valleys but overall: just Julia. I began to think of myself less as "author, author" and more as a word processor. I began to be more willing to let "it," whatever "it" was, write through me. I began to write more quickly. My ego was less invested. Not coincidentally, my career began to lift off.

And so it is, nearly twenty years later, that I find myself passing on the advice that gave me so much freedom: let something, or somebody, or writing itself write through you. Step aside and let the creativity or the Great Creator or, as my sister calls it, the Great Author, do its work through you. In other words, cooperate, don't seek to coopt the power that can enter the world through your hand.

On the days when I drop the rock, on the days when I get over myself, I write freely and happily. My writer's life is a loose garment.

It's my baggy Chinese silk pajamas. It's a life where I—and my brain-children—are allowed to come as they are. Since I'm not invested in looking like a "real" writer or in acting like a "real" writer, I am freed up to have a real life. Since it isn't about concentrating on how smart I am and how brilliant I need to be, since it's now about listening to what is trying to speak through me, I can trust that the flow of writing is always there, always available, just like electricity at the flick of a switch.

This means I can turn my writing off long enough to deal with a family member or friend and that I can flick it back on again. I can put my Muse on hold if something important comes up that must be dealt with. I can lead a life in which my writing is a full partner but not a domineering and jealous spouse. I can have my writing and outside loves and interests. I can allow those loves and interests to feed my work. I can let the world into my work as an active ingredient and not as something that must be held at bay "while I work."

If writing is about the play of ideas, that word "play" must be given more than lip service. Writing has to have some "play" in it like a bridge cable. Writing has to have some "play" in it, like a jump rope. Writing has to have some "play" in it, like the "play" of light across a field when the sky is dappled with clouds. Writing, in other words, must be large enough, loose enough, relaxed enough to contain all the multiplicity of a full life.

Martha, adroit at standing aside to receive information from other realms, often talks to me about the paradox of becoming ourselves through forgetting ourselves. The goal, as she sees it, is to allow our individual self to become subsumed by the larger Self working through us.

"If we really get in the exact moment, if we really just try to remember that the only reality is love, then we can stop worrying about results and just do what we do," Martha says. She herself exemplifies this advice, moving among multiple worlds with ease and grace.

(I think of it as stretching a piece of material so that it becomes so sheer we can see through it.)

When we are willing to become gossamer, to allow the fabric of our own personality to expand and stretch to take in what we can apprehend through fully listening to inspiration, we become both more creative and less invested in the authorship of what we create. Often, we have an experience of awe as we feel what we are creating being born "through" us. The term "brainchildren" becomes more real to us as we experience our creations as entities with lives and agendas of their own. Rather than the "author" of a piece of work, we often experience ourselves as the "midwife" of a piece of work. It is born through us just as our children come through us but are possessed of lives and destinies of their own.

In a sense, our creativity is none of our business. It is a given, not something to be aspired to. It is not an invention of our ego. It is, instead, a natural function of our soul. We are intended to breathe and to live. We are intended to listen and create. We do not need special pens. We do not need special rooms or even special times. What we do need is the intention to allow creativity to create through us. When we open ourselves to something or someone greater than ourselves working through us, we paradoxically open ourselves to our own greatest selves.

BEING AN OPEN CHANNEL
Initiation Tool

For the use of this tool, begin by nudging the door of your mind an inch or two farther open. The tool you are about to try requires a spirit of open-mindedness and scientific inquiry. This is one of my favorite writing tools, one that might be called guided writing or even channeled writing. You may want to think of this as calling on the Muse. You might consider it a time to involve higher forces. You might, on the other hand, prefer to think of it in more Jungian terms: contacting the self.

You may want to use music, incense, sage, or a quiet, rhythmic drum track to help you open up. On the other hand, I have found that the process is really so simple that we do not need to make much ritualized rigamarole around it. If you have been writing Morning Pages, then you have already trained your censor to stand aside and let you enter deeper realms. The trick of this tool is the trick of many children's games: "Let's pretend." Pretend that you are opening to higher realms and, like as not, you will discover that you have.

For this tool, I prefer initially to use a question-and-answer format. Set pen to page and ask a question on which you need advice. There are no wrong or stupid questions, and over time you will learn how to phrase your questions most effectively for you. For example:

Q. What to do about Daniel?

Next listen for advice and write down what you hear.

A. Encourage Daniel, tell him he's on the right track.

Your questions can and should be about anything and everything. You can pursue a line of questioning with greater and greater specificity so that you arrive at some of the root issues you are dealing with.

Q. Does she love me?

A. The issue here lies with your loving yourself.

Q. Yes, but I would feel happier if I knew her true feelings.

A. You must take some direct, concrete, and loving actions on your own behalf.

Q. I want her to nurture me. How can I get her to do that?

A. You must open the door to receiving nurturing by nurturing yourself.

Do not be surprised if your guidance feels stubborn, hardheaded, and practical. You may find yourself the possessor of some previously unacknowledged "tough love" wisdom that you can use in your own behalf. In this regard, your answers to your questions will probably surprise you. Answers very often seem simpler and wiser than our normal thinking. Answers may suggest unorthodox previously unthought-of solutions. It is my experience and that of my students—that the advice is worth trying out.

This is a tool you may use frequently once you become comfortable with it. Many students use it to "drop down the well" for quick guidance and stress relief in work situations. Others cite shifts of focus in career, in relationships, and, of course, in their writing.

Allow yourself to Q. and A. in half-hour sessions initially. Do not be surprised if a great deal of sound advice seems to have been waiting to be tapped into!

INTEGRATING

FOUR DAYS AGO, I took a bad fall off a young horse. The fall was—as they usually are—my fault. I was jumping and I was also "jumping ahead." I was on Bob, my favorite horse, heading around a jump course, but I was actually in the future on the phone with this annoying person who never called as scheduled. Bob, a young horse, felt my absence of focus and lost focus himself. He suddenly swerved, ran out on a fence, and I came off, landing on my left side and ankle.

Days later, my ribs ache sharply and it is difficult to sleep except in certain postures. I feel a sense of empathy for all jockeys and steeplechase riders who have ever taken a header. I suspect my ribs are cracked or badly bruised—there's nothing to be done with "ribs" except time—and in any case their soreness has put me squarely into my body—not a particularly comfortable place but a welcome place nonetheless. I am called upon to stop racing forward and to take stock of where I have been. As is my habit, I do this on the page. Writing is a valuable tool for integration.

The root of the word "integration" is the smaller word "integer," which means "whole." Too often, racing through life, we become the "hole," not the "whole." We become an unexamined maw into which our encounters and experiences rush unassimilated, leaving us both full and unsatisfied because nothing has been digested and taken in.

In order to "integrate" our experiences, we must take them into account against the broader canvas of our life. We must slow down and recognize when currents of change, like movements in a symphony, are moving through us.

Carl is a high-powered television executive. He is at the top of his game at the top of a career mountain that is steep and slippery. Everything is going as any outsider might wish it to go, but to Carl, on the inside, there is a subtle feeling of dissatisfaction, a sense of being out of control.

"I undertook producing as a means to accomplish good in the world," Carl says. "Now I am uncertain that the ratings figures that correspond to my success actually translate to the doing good that I hoped to accomplish."

Carl is in an existential crisis. His inner reality and his outer world no longer mesh. On a daily basis, Carl explores the rift in his value system by writing.

"I put it on the page and I look at it. I do not pretend that I have no discomfort. I do not tell myself that everything is fine. Instead, I explore daily what I can do to move the life I have closer to the life that I want. I explore daily how I can move my choices of what to produce closer to my personal view of what needs to be accomplished on a planetary level. I work to let consciousness and not just commerce guide my decisions. I go to the page as I would to a mentor, asking for guidance and advice on how to proceed."

Carl is integrating his dreams with his reality.

Allison, a woman in her early forties, is newly widowed, having lost her husband swiftly and savagely to cancer.

"Writing is what I am doing about Rob's death. Writing is how I am saying good-bye to him, to our life, to our dreams together. Writing is also how I am trying to say hello to someone new, to the someone that I am without Rob. There are days when I can barely write. There are days when all I do is write. There are days when writing is the only thing that I can hang on to. Without writing, I would not be able to get through this time. Writing is more than a lifeline right now. Right now writing is my life."

Allison is integrating her past with her future.

Writing is a friend whose shoulder we can cry on. Writing is a confidant who listens and lets us sort things out. Writing is a comrade, marching with us through the steep days of sorrow and despair. Writing is our weather and also how we change our weather. Writing is our landscape and how we view the landscape that we have.

I am changing movements in my life symphony right now.

For many years, a relationship has been central to my work and my thought. It has loomed large on my personal horizon, bulking out the rest of the landscape. I think of it as being like the flank of the famous church Georgia O'Keeffe painted, a large monolithic shape that dominated her canvas as it has my life.

For six weeks now, I have been moving my life's lens slowly backward and to the left. I have, in movie terms, pulled focus, backed off from the close-up of the monolith, put it into perspective within a larger context. It is as though I have drawn back from the church flank and dollied left to reveal, "Oh, my! There's a whole village here!"

Putting this to the page, I feel a flow of emotions starting. First, there is grief. I have loved working with this man. I have loved the keen excitement I felt in his presence, in his artistry. Second, there is relief. I had felt dragged off center, stretching myself too far afield sometimes to accommodate his mood swings and abrupt disappearances. Third, there is anger: "How could I have overlooked the toll this collaboration took on my emotional energies? The walking-on-eggshells aspect to it?" Fourth, there is another feeling—curiosity—stirring like grass in the wind. Something new is coming. I can feel it although it is still offscreen.

The fall from the horse, the sudden collision with the reality of hard-packed dirt, it all strikes me as a physical manifestation of my creative shift. In the wake of my creative disengagement, a distancing first personal and later professional, I feel sore, bruised up, slowed down, and as if I need to handle myself with gentle care. Writing helps me to do this. I write to tell myself the truth, the whole truth and nothing but the truth. I write, not to make art, but to make sense. I try my hand, as now, at a poem. I am looking for honesty, not artistry.

I am integrating my emotions with my integrity.

You Were

You were my landscape.
The mountain, the sky.
The valley where I planned
Orchards by and by.
I did not suspect the lava
Simmering beneath the slope.
I did not detect the tremor
Mounting like a bomb
Ticking into birth.
You were my green earth.
When the mountain came apart in pieces,
Its furthest reaches eclipsing the sun,
I still was not certain what had been done.
You were my landscape,
What I took for granted—
All that has slanted skyward,
Falling to earth. Ashes,
Debris and heat, shattered glass,
Broken boards and dirt.
For what it's worth,
I loved you.
Where do we start, as each is,
To pick up the pieces?

Without writing, without writing long enough and deep enough, I would try to move forward as if no fall from grace had happened, as if it were a mere misstep and not a violent smashing of hopes and dreams. I see that like the villager who did not know his peaceful mountain was a volcano, I did not know I was building my creative life on a lava field. What felt firm was not.

Like the villager, I feel betrayed. These are not comfortable feelings, but they are emotional facts, and, like the shards of glass that must be swept from the village square, I must pause, take stock, and clear out this wreckage before I can go forward again.

When we are using writing to do the work of integra
ing is not only the river but often the bridge across the rive
is not only the chasm where we enter in terror to deal with i
ing feelings but also the rope we throw across the chasm, the rope we
use to pull ourselves to safety. The dailiness of writing allows us not
only to walk into change and through it but also to record change in
tiny, manageable increments, to find grounding when our lives feel
unhorsed.

INTEGRATING
Initiation Tool

Very often, without our knowing it, we slip "out of synch" in our
lives. We are subtly out of alignment, off our center, and it happened
without our noticing. At times like this, we need help integrating,
coming back into a whole. The following tool, though very simple, is
remarkably effective at moving us "back on our spine."

Set aside fifteen minutes. Set pen to page and number from one
to twenty-five. Then, very rapidly complete the phrase "I wish"
twenty-five times. Your wishes will range from the small to the substantial, from the personal to the professional. For example:

1. I wish my hair were longer.
2. I wish my sister lived closer.
3. I wish I had a piano teacher.
4. I wish I were running daily.
5. I wish my novel would gel.
6. I wish I had more cash flow.
7. I wish I were less depressed.
8. I wish I had new pots and pans.
9. I wish I had a date for New Year's.
10. I wish I had better secretarial help.

Wish lists are more potent than they appear. Written out once a
month, they actually move us on a subconscious level to act in the di-

rection of our dreams. It is my experience that the mere act of putting wishes on the page begins to put them into motion. First you wish you were exercising a little more, then you find yourself walking a little more briskly. First you wish you were listening to more classical music, then you find yourself buying a boxed set of Vivaldi. Write your wish list out, date it, and save it. Repeat this exercise once a month or whenever you are feeling particularly scattered.

CREDIBILITY

THE DAY IS GRAY. The atmosphere is heavy and oppressive. A storm is coming in. My mood matches. This is a hard day to write. This is a day when my censor is awake, alert, and active, responding to the incoming storm with ominous hissing and aggression—the way snakes in a reptile house grow restless when the barometer drops.

"You've got nothing to say," my censor hisses. "What you think you have to say hasn't been said before and better? Who do you think you are, trying to write a book about writing?" This is the same helpful fellow who used to tell me, when I was a newspaper columnist, that the man at the security desk would not believe my ID and let me in to write because I "didn't look like a real writer." (Whatever *that* looked like.)

I call this the "credibility attack" and it is a familiar one. All writers suffer credibility attacks; learning to ignore them is part of surviving as a writer. Based on the idea that writing is product, not process, the credibility attack wants to know just what credits you've amassed lately. The mere act of writing, the fact of which makes you a writer, counts for nothing with this monster. The work you do and the fact that you've done it doesn't matter. What matters is where your passport has been stamped. What matters is who says you're a writer besides yourself.

America is a product-oriented country. If we tell someone we wrote a novel, their most common response is not "How wonderful!" but "Do you have a publisher yet?" In other words, will it be a book and will you make any money from it? If it gets published, if you make money, then there is the next question, "So how is your book doing? Has it made any of the best-seller lists?"

Writing for the sake of writing, writing that draws its credibility from its very existence, is a foreign idea to most Americans. As a culture, we want cash on the barrel head. We want writing to earn dollars and sense so that it makes sense to us. We have a conviction—which is naive and misplaced—that being published has to do with being "good" while not being published has to do with being "amateur." We treat the unpublished writer as though he or she suffers an embarrassing case of unrequited love. We say things like "You may not want to put all your eggs into one basket." And "You might want something to fall back on." Books proliferate on what we "should" write and how we can "write for the market." There's not much advice along the lines of "Write what would make you happy." There is something patently foolish, it would seem, in doing something just for the love of it.

This morning I had breakfast with a woman who said to me, "I'm not a real writer."

"What do you mean by that?" I asked.

"Oh, I write all the time and have since I was a little kid and I do it almost daily and I think of it as being my best friend, but I'm not a professional writer," she replied.

This was a sophisticated woman, a spiritual adroit, a woman whose consciousness had escaped many of the nets and snares of group-think and yet, and still, although she wrote constantly and happily, she was not, in her mind, a real writer.

"My grammar is why I'm not a writer," another woman who writes all the time told me. "I love to write and I write little stories and poems and occasionally an article, but I don't really know anything about the rules and so I'd hardly think of myself as a writer."

I thought of the articles I had read under this woman's name, the letters I had received and enjoyed, the fact that she had "fooled" me.

Until I heard her reservations I would always have thought of her as a writer.

"I can't spell to save my life," yet another woman told me. "I love to write but with spelling like mine, I'm sure I can't take it very seriously."

The woman with the "bad" spelling actually suffers from a reading disorder, dyslexia, and her love of writing has persisted despite obstacles.

"Just use spell check," I told her. "Or even just a dictionary. After you write something, check it over. It doesn't matter if you 'can't' spell. We've got computer programs to do it for you."

"But isn't that cheating?" the woman wondered—as if writing were some circus trick that she had failed to master and any help, any "net" took away the glory of the stunt.

"I suppose I'm a writer, but I'm just a business writer," a man recently told me. "I write pamphlets on how to do things. I don't really think that counts."

Why doesn't it count? Writing clearly and well on how to do something is one of the most difficult forms of writing that I've ever encountered. What makes it less "writing" than a short story? Where does this pecking order come from? This notion of "real" writing and "other" writing? This notion of hierarchy, writing that is "art" being a higher form of writing than writing that is merely artful?

"I think if I ever got published, then I would believe I was a writer," a student tells me.

Maybe and maybe not. The credibility attack has been known to be cunning and baffling, raising its bar to keep pace with a burgeoning career.

"You may have written one good book, but that's all you've got in you."

"It was a fluke they took that article."

"Sooner or later they'll figure out that you don't have what it really takes to sustain a column."

Writing for the love of writing, the sheer act of writing, is the only antidote for the poison of a credibility attack—and the antidote is short-lived and must be readministered.

write today?"

ou're a writer today."

d be lovely if being a writer were a permanent state that we could attain to. It's not, or if it is, the permanence comes posthumously.

A page at a time, a day at a time, is the way we must live our writing lives. Credibility lies in the act of writing. That is where the dignity is. That is where the final "credit" must come from.

CREDIBILITY
Initiation Tool

Credibility is closely tied to our sense of personal worthiness. The tool that follows is an invaluable aid to personal self-worth and credibility. Both of those qualities can make it a little easier to move onto the page. Again, remember that in order to do self-expression, we need to have a self to express. This tool aims at strengthening your sense of self.

For this tool, you probably will need to set aside two blocks of writing time, each one and a half hours or a little longer. (Some students, but not many, do manage this tool in one sitting. Most find they need a breather midway through.)

Retreat to a calm and quiet writing corner. You may want to light a candle, burn incense, and cue up some soothing music. Setting pen to page, number from one to one hundred. Go back through your life and list a full one hundred things you are proud of. These do not need to be what you should be proud of or what other people may tell you you should be proud of. Some of what you're proud of may even be antisocial or even illegal. It's your list. Let yourself be particular and personal. For example, I'm proud of:

1. Teaching Domenica to ride
2. Staging my musical *Avalon*
3. Telling off the sixth-grade bully
4. Writing my three novellas

5. Growing my hair long
6. Reconnecting with Daniel
7. Working with Tim
8. Walking my dogs daily
9. Writing my dad often
10. Nurturing long-term friendships

Think of this tool as a private résumé. It will help point you in directions that have genuine meaning in your own value system. This tool is a potent defense against credibility attacks, as it reminds us firmly that our credibility is a spiritual, not material, issue.

PLACE

I BEGAN MY WRITING LIFE in the upstairs corner bedroom of my parents' house. It was a small room. The dresser, desk, and bed were painted white. The curtains, gingham, were lilac and white checked. (I write in a lilac room with white curtains today.) In that gingham room I wrote my early poems and short stories dedicated to the intention of winning Peter Mundy's heart.

My writing life moved after that down to the basement, my high school hangout. There was an upright piano, a poker table, a battered couch and chairs. In the basement half-light, I wrote high school journalism, poems, and more short stories. I wanted the attention of John Kane, and I got it.

When I went to college, my writing life began to occupy a cranny high up in Georgetown Library under the nose of a saturnine gargoyle, my critic incarnate. Poems, papers, and short stories unfurled beneath his baleful gaze.

When my parents became ill, I went back to Libertyville, Illinois, to care for them, and my writing life moved into a bilevel phase: the basement, again, where I wrote early *Rolling Stone* pieces, and my brother Jaimie's bedroom, where I pursued a diet of apples, cheddar cheese, and J&B scotch while I wrote *Morning,* a (very) youthful novel. I used an old Olympia typewriter. Its body was the same trench-coat tan as my current computer.

When my parents recovered, my writing life and I moved back to Washington, D.C. Now I wrote in black and white speckled notebooks, in cafés, and parks, on a small schoolroom desk in front of a barred apartment window, on trains and in waiting rooms. My writing life, like my life itself, was becoming portable. I was hired as a mail sorter for *The Washington Post* and began writing there on long sheets of carboned paper rolled through heavy electric typewriters. My journalism career began.

That career took me to hotel rooms around the country, where I wrote on yellow legal pads or rented typewriters and rigged them up to write on card tables near the window of whatever was passing as the view. Flying to and from assignments, I discovered the joy of writing on airplanes, getting down page after page as we shot through a tunnel of time.

For a while I carried a black leather blank-sheet book and I sketched the locations in which I wrote. I seemed to be using the sketches like Polaroids: I was here doing this. I did not know then what I know now, that for me a sense of place is central to good writing.

I am thinking back to high school. We have been assigned to read *The Scarlet Letter.* I find the book boring despite its adultery. I find particularly annoying the long passages about nightfall and burning sticks and the way the light fell or didn't fall against the moors. It is now thirty years later and what I remember of *The Scarlet Letter* is not Hester Prynne's plight but those images of flickering firelight dancing on the moors.

In the early seventies, during Watergate, I wrote for *Rolling Stone.* I remember Hunter Thompson saying to me, "The secret to good writing, Julia, lies in taking good notes. I take great notes."

"Taking great notes" is another way of saying "place matters." When we place a piece of writing carefully and specifically ("I am writing this on a sunny spring morning with sun streaming through a white lace curtain and a lilac bush blooming against the window"), we create a context for what we are saying. We allow the reader to bring in a world of powerful associations and discriminations that makes the reader-writer dance far more intimate.

The specificity of a writer's detail, the willingness to disclose detail, allows or bars intimacy. Place is the most pivotal fact of connection. We acknowledge this obliquely when we say "Where are you at?" If I tell you literally where I am at, you will connect to a grounded sense of "where I am at." If I say, for example, that the walls to my writing room are pastel iris and that there are wreaths of dried flowers and Indian corn on the walls, you will know that I am a romantic and a lover of nature and so even my most hard-bitten prose passages will be colored by your accurate perception of my more tender side.

If I tell you I keep an altar in my writing room, that the altar features two porcelain theater dolls that represent my daughter and myself, then you will know that no matter how hip my short stories may appear, they were written by someone who values family and is old-fashioned beneath her modernity. If I add that right next to my computer is a framed baby picture of my now-twenty-one-year-old daughter, you will begin to factor in that I am also somewhat sentimental—a variable offset, perhaps, by the presence of a green lizard on my altar, the symbol of change.

The accumulation of details, the willingness to be specific and precise, the willingness to "place" a piece of writing accurately in context—all of these things make for writing that a reader can connect to. Perhaps more important than that, it makes for writing that the writer can connect to. Naming our experience accurately and intimately, we claim it as our own. It becomes our territory, somewhere we really were, someplace we have feelings about. Once we contact the flow of deeper feelings under the skein of details, we have a chance at writing that touches something deeper than the surface in us and in those who read.

"We are born in a certain time and a certain place," wrote Carl Jung regarding astrology, "and like vintage wines we retain the flavor of our origins."

The same may be said of a piece of writing.

I began writing my novella *Between Heaven and Earth* in a hotel room in Boulder, Colorado. I had just separated from my creative partner, Tim Wheater, who was off for several months incommunicado in the Australian bush.

"Write us something where we can stay in character," he had said in leaving.

I propped myself against the pillow in a vintage Victorian bedroom and, looking out the window at a week of snow, I began to write love letters between a husband and a wife. Wheater was in sunny and hot Australia. I placed the husband in sunny and hot Vietnam. I was in the chill, wintry landscape of the far western great plains, literally a half-mile from the mountains where the plains ended, and so I placed the wife in Kansas, where there were no mountains—after all, the snow was cutting off my view of them as well.

Wheater had departed abruptly, leaving me in charge of a joint creative project. I gave the wife twin boys, approximately the same weight of responsibility that I felt overburdened trying to handle. I had trouble with managing the creative crew Wheater had left behind. I made the boys rambunctious and out of control without their father.

The wife worries about her husband's proximity to Vietnamese brothels. The Boulderado Hotel, where I was writing, was itself an old frontier brothel. The wife had a stern, antisensual bedroom. It was directly taken from the room I was staying in myself. Bit by bit, detail by detail, event by event, I translated life as I was living it—sharing it and not sharing it—into life between a husband and a wife. The dead wet leaves of Boulder became the dead wet leaves of a small Kansas town. The misery and loneliness of a creative project left half finished became the misery and loneliness of a household left unhusbanded. I could not change the facts of my life, but I could transform those facts into art and an art made much more artful by the inclusion of place.

As I write this essay, the sunny spring morning has shifted and great gray clouds bulk overhead. Yesterday was for me a sunny day. I had a long and lovely conversation with a new and cherished friend. Today the distance between us hangs over my landscape like the clouds over Taos Valley. Last night at twilight we had an abrupt hailstorm. Today my lilacs are still blooming—despite the odds.

Fact: I, too, am blooming despite the odds.

Fact: The long winter is over despite the hail.

Fact: Four songbirds are balancing on the feeder just outside the study window. Tails tipping in the wind, they ride the feeder like a swing. A shaft of sun breaks the clouds. They sing in a sunny place.

PLACE
Initiation Tool

When we write, we "place" ourselves in our world. We say, "This is where I am, right now, and this is how I feel about that." Conversely, when we focus on the places where we have been, we often connect to a deep and specific sense of how we felt when we were there. In other words, by mapping our literal, physical placements, we are often able to more accurately map our psychological placement. Good writers—and good writing teachers—know this. I am thinking specifically of the grounded, place-oriented writings and teachings of Natalie Goldberg. When I think of this tool, I always think of her, writing in cafés and encouraging her students to do the same.

The tool that follows is one I prefer to do "out." Set aside an hour's writing time and take yourself out of the house and off to a café, restaurant, library, or some other foreign place to work. First, set pen to page and list every single place you have ever lived. For some of you this will be only a few locales. For others, it will be a list of dozens.

After you have listed any and all places, choose one that brings back particularly vivid memories. Writing in the first person, in the present tense, put yourself back into the place and time you lived there. For one half hour, allow yourself to write out the reality of this younger self. For example:

"I am nineteen years old, a junior in college, and I am living alone on the top floor of a frame house on Adee Avenue in the Bronx. The apartment has three rooms—a little living room, a bedroom, a kitchen, and a bathroom. The windows of this apartment have a large tree just outside. Squirrels scamper along the tree limbs and come close enough to stare in the windows and watch me as I write. I am frightened, alone, and trying to be brave. I love it that when my windows are open you can smell freshly baked Italian bread from the bakery half a block away. . . ."

This is a powerful and emotional exercise that you may wish to return to repeatedly each time, choosing to "place" yourself in a different place. Writing work such as this, while sometimes deeply felt, yields us a sense of continuity and a profound connection to the sense of adventure in our own storyteller's story.

HAPPINESS

Y O U K N O W T H E picture: the writer as a tormented soul, writing from angst, writing from pain, writing from alienation. Cigarette clenched in tight lips, shot glass just at the elbow, the writer is writing from anger, writing from outrage, writing from indignation. Writers do write for those reasons, but they write for many others. Not the least of these is joy:

JERUSALEM IS WALKING IN THIS WORLD

This is a great happiness.
The air is silk.
There is milk in the looks
That come from strangers.
I could not be happier
If I were bread and you could eat me.

Joy is dangerous.
It fills me with secrets.
"Yes" hisses in my veins.
The pains I take to hide myself
Are sheer as glass.
Surely this will pass—

The wind like kisses,
The music in the soup,
The group of trees laughing
As I say their names.

It is all hosannah.
It is all prayer.
Jerusalem is walking in this world.
Jerusalem is walking in this world.

When I wrote that poem, I was dizzy with happiness. I was mid-way through a book tour with composer Tim Wheater and he had suggested we make a poetry album together. We were crisscrossing America giving concerts and poetry readings, introducing my book *The Vein of Gold* and Wheater's album *Heartland*. Our work was being well received, our friendship was blossoming, and there was even time to visit with friends as we toured.

I loved Wheater's music, had wanted to tour with him for years, and I found the process of the dream come true sufficient to light my heart like a candle burning at both ends. I was astonished by the depth of my creative joy and, as I do with everything, I turned to the page, writing. The album idea was Wheater's solution to a joyous problem: We had to do something with the poems that were flowing out of me, sometimes as many as three a day. "How shrewd of me, touring with a Muse," I would joke.

I am not the only writer who writes from sheer joy. My friend Natalie Goldberg remarks, "The deepest secret in our heart of hearts is that we are writing because we love the world."

How many more books might get written if we believed that writers could write out of love, out of glee, out of bliss—or even out of simple fondness? What if we wrote letters to the editor or to Congress to express our pleasure with the way some things were going?

It is my belief that writing is a way to bless and to multiply our blessings. I cherish letters, postcards, faxes, notes, and even Post-its from my friends. We are so skilled in the art of negative imagination, we are so adroit at the art of writing out of anxiety, what might our writing and our world look like if we allowed ourselves to inhabit our positive imagination?

I am in the process of falling in love. It feels less like "falling" and more like "rising up" than I remember. Maybe because I am older, twice divorced, a long time single, this new love catches me by surprise and finds me moving toward it not with the glee of a skater whizzing across a glassy pond but like a cautious shore dweller afraid to venture onto thin ice. And yet . . .

The man I am starting to love is tall and kind and funny. He is an incredibly precise and whimsical writer who veers off into sudden flights of fancy. I am not used to whimsy in a man. I am mesmerized. I watch him like TV. "Now what?" I ask, catching some new shenanigans that are pure fun, pure folly.

Now what? I am writing.

UNPREPARED

I.

I'm not prepared for this.
I can't pronounce this bliss.
The way we flow,
The knowing where to go—
This ebb and flow—
Can't we take it slow?
Where are the walls?
The shadows in the halls?
This light—can it be right?
Where does it come from?
I've known a different sun,
Walked a different earth,
Where air was used for grieving—
I think—we are leaving.

II.

Before we met
I knew your face
From stars and flowers.

I knew your name
From wind and grasses.
Before we met,
The red earth held my heart,
The sky cradled my dreams,
The forest floor was my green bed.
These were what I wed before we met.
Now that you are here
I am wed to galaxies.
Our sky does not contain me.
Our sun is a candle to what I see.
Sheer as cliff, the walls drop away.

Real life is persistent in its capacity to bring happiness. It is difficult, even on the most miserable of days, not to grudgingly notice something that speaks of an enjoyable world. I am thinking now of a day in the dead of winter when I was living in Manhattan. I was suffering from a terrible cold. My daughter was suffering from a terrible cold. We were housebound, miserable, sniping at each other.

"Let's go for a little walk," I suggested.

"Why?"

"Just let's."

We bundled into winter coats. We took extra wads of Kleenex. We made it out to the cold, crisp streets. On one corner, a West Highland terrier bedeviled his owner by disappearing under the table, where a hat and scarf and glove salesman was hawking his wares. At the next corner, twin brown-eyed babies giggled excitedly over a silky spaniel who was just their height. We passed two British lovers squabbling pleasantly over what dreadful American movie to see. We stopped to admire some summer necklaces laid out in the chill December light. We passed a tiny, aged lady, minked to her toes, clinging to the arm of her taller daughter, a glacial blonde.

"If you think I'm going to take care of you when you're a little old lady," my daughter snarled playfully, drawing my own arm through hers.

What was going on? We had started our walk so miserable, so solid in our misery, and here was happiness creeping in without any real encouragement, creeping in a step at a time as we walked. Even Scrooge would notice.

Just as walking aerobicizes the physical body, producing a flow of endorphins and good feelings, writing seems to alter the chemical balance of the soul itself, restoring balance and equilibrium when we are out of sorts, bringing clarity, a sense of right action, a feeling of purpose to a rudderless day. Furthermore, writing when we are out of happiness can lead us into writing from happiness. We recall happier moments and we recall happiness itself.

Writing is a form of cherishing. Counting back over the tiny marvels of that wintry Manhattan day, seeing the sunny Caribbean sparkle of the faux jewels laid out on the sidewalk card table, I was struck by the exuberant optimism of vendors making their livelihood from the street stalls of "leather lane" in London to these in Manhattan.

"Look at this necklace. I just made it this morning," the vendor cajoled. He fingered a necklace the colors of a Caribbean vacation. He glowed with self-satisfaction over the beauty of his craft. He liked the series of choices—blue next to green, silver, not gold—that led to his finished product. He reminded me of a writer, pleased by a well-polished paragraph.

"I just string words together," we writers say. We finger words like beads, choosing one over the other.

Writing, like jewelry design, is a series of choices that lead to a sense of something made—that something is "sense." Sense brings to the writer choice and, with choice, a sense of at least the potential for happiness.

Two variables seem essential for life to feel beneficent. One variable is stability. The other is change. Writing supplies a sense of both variables. Writing both gives continuity and creates a sense of continuity. Writing both gives change and creates an awareness of change. A writing life is therefore—far from what our mythology around writing tells us—very often a life with substantial happiness at its core. Writing to find my happiness, I find my happiness—writing.

HAPPINESS
Initiation Tool

Although our negative mythology around writing tells us that writers are often depressed and tormented creatures, the truth is that too much torment and too much depression can make it as difficult to write as to make the bed, wash the dishes, do the laundry. To the depressed person, writing may present itself as one more chore. For this reason, we are actually working on our writing when we directly address the larger issue of our happiness.

Set aside one full hour. Draw yourself a hot bath. Add bubbles. Light a few candles, perhaps a stick of incense. Cue up some beloved music, get in the steamy bath, and simply soak. Let your thoughts float like bubbles. Let them slip and drift, then, gently and consciously turn to listing things that make you happy. Towel off. Race to the page. Number from one to fifty. List fifty things that make you happy.

1. Motown
2. The Evening Star
3. Godiva chocolate
4. The Beatles
5. A good sunset
6. Horses
7. Neruda poetry
8. Cinnamon ice cream
9. New York pizza
10. Running
11. Etc.

Happiness is not only a mood. It is a decision. Writing our list of fifty happinesses causes us to see how simple some forms of joy are, how we can make ourselves happy in simple ways—read the Neruda poems, eat the ice cream, take time to check out the sunsets. Happiness lists are also an effective deterrent for situational depression. When the blues set in, the simple act of listing joys can help elicit some.

MAKING IT

THE OTHER AFTERNOON, a young writer came over for homemade pie, a walk through the sagebrush, and a conversation about writing. Young, handsome, as dashing as F. Scott Fitzgerald in tennis whites, the young writer looked like central casting's idea of the Young Writer. He was excited. As we set off across the sage fields, dogs in tow, he told me he had two newly minted short stories, a small crisp article, and high hopes . . . except for one thing: what were his odds of "making it" as a writer?

"Julia, I'd love to write, to be a writer, but I'm afraid I have no talent. Or not enough talent anyway."

"What's enough talent? Don't worry about talent. Just write. Remember what director Martin Ritt said?"

"No. I'm afraid I don't."

"Ritt said, 'I don't have much respect for talent. It's what you do with it that counts.'"

"Ah. How do you keep from getting muddy on these walks?"

"You can't keep from getting muddy."

"Ah."

The Young Writer's tennis whites were getting spattered around the edges. He was walking carefully, as incongruous as someone in dress whites on a battlefield. Around us the dogs leaped and whirled, slathered with mud, having the time of their lives.

It is interesting to me that we ask a question about the writing life that we do not ask about other professions. For example, we do not say, "What are your odds of making it as an investment banker? As an elementary-school teacher? As a chemist?"

In those, and most professions, we assume that an interest in pursuing the career implies a probable proclivity for it and a reasonable chance for success. Not so with writing. The truth is, when you want a writing career and are willing to do the work to get it, the odds work with you, not against you. This is simple metaphysical law. As Goethe advised us, "Whatever you think you can do or believe you can do, begin it—for action has magic grace and power in it."

I quoted Goethe to the young writer.

"You make it sound so simple!"

"It is simple."

"But don't you have to know the right people, that kind of thing?"

"No."

"Really?"

"Really. If you write and write well, the 'right' people will eventually want to know you. So don't try to meet people. Try writing."

"That feels so—"

"Practical? Do-able?"

"Harsh."

"Because it gives you back your power?"

"Maybe."

"Because there's no one to blame but yourself?"

"Heh. Don't sugar-coat it! In other words, in order to be a writer, try writing?"

"That's my formula."

"It would be!"

The Young Writer was laughing. He could appreciate the irony of his tennis whites and the messy practical advice that I was giving him.

"The minute you start writing, your odds of being a writer start to run one hundred percent more in your favor: you are already a writer. You're writing, aren't you?"

"Yes, but—"

"But?"

"But what about publishing?"

"If you keep writing, you'll publish. If you keep focusing on publishing, you may not write."

"But what if I write forever and I never publish?"

"Hasn't happened yet."

"But it could."

"Every piece you write makes your being published more likely."

"Your solution to everything is 'just write'!"

"That's true."

The Young Writer was annoyed. He could see that all roads were leading him straight back to his desk, where, sooner or later, he would "just have to write."

"I'm scared to submit things," he finally said.

"Everybody's scared to submit things. The trick is to keep writing and submit while you're writing. Don't stop and wait for a response. Keep up your momentum."

The word "momentum" hung between us. I could sympathize with the Young Writer's wanting an outward sign, an aid to his momentum. Unlike him, I was certain it would come. His own commitment would trigger it. For thirty years now I have watched my own and others' commitments trigger positive opportunities in the world. I have even found a quote that accurately describes the phenomena I've observed.

Mountain climber William Hutchinson Murray, who mounted expeditions "against the odds," had this to say about the whole question of odds, pro and con our endeavors:

"Concerning all acts of initiative or creation, there is one elementary truth, the ignorance of which kills countless ideas and splendid plans: that the moment one definitely commits oneself, then Providence moves too."

"Then Providence moves too": that's the telling line. First we must commit, then the universe follows the direction pointed by our commitment. Over and over in my teaching life, I hear stories of synchronicity: "I just finished the short story, when I went to a party and met this guy who was starting a literary magazine," or "I just decided

I would love writing about the arts, when I heard that the arts columnist at our local paper had moved back east . . ."

We commit, then the Universe commits. We are the cause, the Universe delivers the effect. We act internally and the Universe acts externally. Again this is where so many of us fall into a false sense of powerlessness. "If I were published, then I'd be a real writer," we tell ourselves. "What are the odds of my being published?"

Your odds of being published become one hundred percent the minute you are willing to self-publish. My book *The Artist's Way*, which has now sold well over a million books, began life as a self-published manuscript. So did my book, *The Money Drunk*. So did my short story collection, *Popcorn*. I am, perhaps, more stubborn than most or maybe more uppity or maybe just more convinced of the essential democracy of the arts. I believe that if one of us cares enough to write something, someone else will care enough to read it. We are all in this together, I believe, and our writing and reading one another is a powerful comfort to us all.

The universe is not, to my eye, a cruel and capricious place. I believe that our desire to write is a deep-seated human drive to communicate and that it is answered by an equally powerful human drive to be communicated to. In other words, for every writer there is a reader—or many readers.

We had been trudging for some minutes in silence while I thought about how good the Young Writer's odds were and he thought about exactly the opposite. Finally he spoke:

"But, Julia, how will I ever make any money as a writer?"

"You'll write and get paid for it."

"You make it sound so simple."

"Think of it like making a chair. You make a chair and someone buys it. You write something and someone buys it."

"Making a chair is different from writing."

"Why? Don't make it any different."

"You're too practical."

"I can't afford to make writing a big deal. I like to do it too much and, besides, it is how I make my living. Anything else gets too tangled—don't you think?"

"I think all the time and that's the problem!"

My afternoon's walk with my friend the Young Writer was turning out to be an afternoon of listening to the most common and persuasive blocks that writers in our culture endure. As we tramped on through the sagebrush, keeping one alert eye out for rattlers, the villainous hisses that sounded were instead those of our culture's beliefs about artists.

Mark Bryan calls this the "Edgar Allan Poe school of writing: Live in torment and die broke in the gutter." Some people do, but that fact may have more to do with their untreated alcoholism than their writerly ambitions.

Maybe it was the exercise. Maybe it was my undaunted optimism on his behalf, but the Young Writer was brightening just a little.

"You really think I could make a living as a writer?"

"Writers get paid just like other people get paid. A piece of writing is a piece of work. People pay to have it done the same way they pay to have a dress made or an architectural drawing rendered. And in much the same way that an architect loves to draw and draws things, paid or not, and a seamstress loves to sew and may occasionally whip up a dress for sheer love, a writer is someone who first of all writes and secondly happens to be paid for it."

"Well, I haven't been paid for any writing yet."

"But you will."

"It's nice one of us is sure about that."

It is a very American notion that being paid to do something makes us somehow more legitimate. We would actually do well to take a cue here from the world of sports and realize that just as some of our best athletes are our amateurs, some of our most gifted writers may be too. They may never choose to "go professional."

"But, Julia, I keep thinking how much it means to me to be actually published," the Young Writer said. We were headed home now, back toward blackberry pie, herbal tea for him, and strong coffee for me.

"Of course you want to be published," I said. "So make a list of every place you can think of that may need writers and also commit to publishing yourself."

"Publishing myself?"

"What's wrong with that?"

"I guess I want someone else to say I'm a writer."

"Henry Miller self-published. Walt Whitman self-published."

"Yeah. But they're Henry Miller and Walt Whitman!"

"They weren't yet."

If we keep thinking about how nice it would be to be published by other people, we are leaching ourselves of power. Instead, we need to decide that we will, one, write no matter what and, two, share that writing no matter what.

Instead of thinking in terms of traditional publication, it serves us to think of putting the work out into the world in as many formats and venues as suggest themselves. It is also true that the moment one commits to self-publishing, the work that is so valued seems to take on added values to other publishers as well. (It's a little like the girl with a boyfriend seeming more desirable because of it, I'm afraid.)

I live in a small mountain town, Taos, New Mexico. Writers here hold readings. They get together in living rooms and small cafés and read to each other. They hold open mikes and poetry slams. They run off copies of their stories at Copy Queen, our Xerox establishment, and they mail them out and hand them out. They post their writing on the Web. Not coincidentally, Taos has spawned quite successful small presses, carrying the "just do it, just print it" philosophy one step further.

"But, Julia, my whole family thinks I am nuts."

Now we were in the homestretch—and down to the brass tacks of why so many people find it hard to write. We do not believe we have the "right" to write. We believe that our life experience, overlapping as it does with that of our families and intimates, is somehow not our material.

Families typically display a certain understandable reticence in endorsing writing careers. For one thing, they sense quite accurately that they are part of our material—not necessarily a comfortable position! Secondly, families, despite their many flaws and foibles, do in all probability love us and they have listened to as much negative propaganda about the writing life as we have. Wanting us to "succeed," they want us to pick something we can succeed at and—here's the mythology again—we're told that it's "very tough" in the writing game.

What our mythology doesn't tell us is that there is joy in playing the game you like. Just as a swimmer should swim because the water feels like home to him and a field hockey player should let himself run because his legs like to run, writers need to write because, put simply, it makes us happy. Writing feels good.

B ut, Julia, writing as a life seems so self-indulgent."

My friend the Young Writer had himself in a double whammy. On the one hand, he believed that the odds are stacked against him and that the writing life was tough. On the other hand, he enjoyed writing and felt that constituted a good reason not to let himself do it; it was just too self-indulgent, too decadent.

It strikes me as interesting that if someone loved banking, he wouldn't chastise or castigate himself for choosing that life. If some-one loved history and wanted a life as a history professor, that would be a socially acceptable choice, although it is, in fact, every bit as self-indulgent as doing anything else you love—writing, for example.

Then, too, there is this question: what's wrong with being self-indulgent? Where—and the answer is our Calvinist, Puritan her-itage—do we get the idea that doing what we like is somehow wrong? Often, doing what we like is somehow very right.

I gave the Young Writer blackberry pie and herbal tea. He thanked me for the visit and headed back into town. I headed back to my desk, happy to practice—happier to practice than to preach.

MAKING IT
Initiation Tool

T his tool asks you to take a small step toward declaring yourself a writer. You will need to set aside an hour of writing time, preferably "out" rather than in. Go to a café, order a cup of tea, coffee, a soda or cappuccino. You will be writing two letters. The first letter is from your Inner Writer to you. The second letter is from you to your Inner Writer.

Using this tool will give you a chance to air your fears and grievances. It will also give you a chance to offer reassurance and make plans. Your writer might want to go to open mike poetry evenings but needs the assurance that you'll allow some evenings of being just audience before calling on your writer to perform. Your writer may be worried about spelling and need the assurance you'll use a dictionary or your computer program's spell check. The grammar-phobic Inner Writer may need a promise that you'll purchase *The Elements of Style* for boning up.

Your letter to your writer is a chance for your kindly adult self to be reassuring and practical. More than anything else, the part of us that writes needs support, reassurance, and encouragement. We can offer these ourselves. When we do, our writer responds by taking to the page more happily. The dialogue you are setting up with this tool is another practice that can become a regular part of your writer's repertoire. Whenever you feel stuck or stymied, a check-in with your Inner Writer can often tell you why. Knowing the "why," you can work on how to undo it.

HONESTY

THIS AFTERNOON I RECEIVED a manuscript in the mail. It was bulky, hand-xeroxed, and compulsively readable. It was a love story, written in alternating voices by a husband-and-wife team. He is Kenny Loggins. She is his wife, Julia. Their story is intensely romantic and is told in such intimate detail that I found myself reading and saying to myself, "I am astounded that they have written this book. It is so . . . intimate. It is so . . . brave. It is so—oh, my God! They're talking about that?!"

Because the book is intimate, because the book is brave, because the book is handmade—journal entries, lyric scraps, regulation story-telling prose—the book raises a number of interesting questions. Chief among them the idea that so many of us have that our lives, our personal stories, do not really matter and are not important enough to be the stuff of books.

Kenny Loggins is a very gifted and famous songwriter, but he writes of publishing his book, "Even though I have been a song-writer for thirty years, I've never been more proud of myself. This is one of those 'why you were born moments . . .'"

I am inclined to agree with him.

The Logginses' book is personally risky, stuffed to the gills with autobiographical revelations and resolves. It is a dual self-portrait, not a particularly flattering one, and an all the more lovable one because

of its excruciating candor. Reading this book with its flat-out sincer-
ity and heartfelt go-for-broke truth-telling, I find myself thinking,
"This is what writing is supposed to be about. This is the kind of risk
that makes writing—and reading—appeal to me after all these years."

Writing is about honesty. It is almost impossible to be honest and
boring at the same time. Being honest may be many other things—
risky, scary, difficult, frightening, embarrassing, and hard to do—but
it is not boring. Whenever I am stuck in a piece of writing, I ask
myself, "Am I failing to tell the truth? Is there something I am not
saying, something I am afraid to say?"

When the answer is yes, the writing shows it. There is a softness,
a tentativeness, a rot to it that telling the truth instantly dispels. Telling
the truth on the page, like telling the truth in a relationship, always
takes you deeper.

This week I got to watch myself in some very uncomfortable
ways. A friend of mine sent me a fax that talked about "real artists"
and the other kind. I found myself reacting with real rage: how dare
this friend lecture me about "real artists," and what was a real artist
anyway? I fired off an indignant fax back.

"_____ you," my fax said. "I hate all this pecking order . . ."

That was true—as far as it went. Where it didn't go was far
enough to leave me feeling clean. Overnight, I found myself with a
lingering sense of personal malaise. Something was really bothering
me. The something that was bothering me was the idea that in some
people's eyes, and perhaps my friend's, I might not be a real artist.
This friend's opinion really mattered to me.

Once I admitted that I currently just didn't feel hip and that it still
mattered to me that I feel hip and seem hip, I was able to fax my
friend. "Sorry about overreacting," I wrote. "It's just that I have had
to learn to live a different artist's life than the terminally hip kind." I
went on to explain about writing as a single mother, not being able to
go on location, having to learn to fit in my writing between chores,
being a writer and still showing up for the PTA, writing for *Miami
Vice,* and, on the other hand, for *Redbook.*

Writing that, I saw that as much as I pooh-poohed it, there was
still some part of me that wanted to be hip, slick, cool, and totally
clichéd as an artist. There was a part of me that wanted back every

Camel straight I had ever smoked, every pair of tight jeans and ratty cowboy boots. A mother, a teacher, somebody who writes prayer books, I still carried a part of me that wanted to get my passport stamped "Groovy," and that was a stamp of approval I was evidently still not giving to myself.

Now, none of this was welcome news to me. Blowing up at my friend made me feel foolish—and may have damaged our budding friendship. Admitting that appearances still mattered to me was humbling and not welcome news. On the other hand, I notice that this evening I am a little more comfortable with myself and a lot more comfortable with my writing. (On the other hand, I am writing in a black lace shirt, black leather vest, and black silk pants, so maybe admitting to my racy side let it out of the bag a bit.)

"Do you swear to tell the truth, the whole truth, and nothing but the truth?" that is probably the vow that writers should take, declaring ourselves as committed to honesty as doctors are to healing. For writers—for all of us—honesty is healing, and one of the first things it heals is our prose problems.

When we are telling the truth about how we feel and what we see, we find very precise language with which to do it. Words do not fail us. When we are disguising to ourselves and others the exact nature of what we thought or how we felt, our prose goes mushy along with our thinking. (There are three adjectives where one would do, a few fluffy sentences where a simple fact could well have sufficed.)

Honesty is not only the best policy in writing, it is the only policy that holds up over the long haul. Just as it is exhausting and destructive to lie in our personal lives, it is equally damaging to do it in our writing. And because we have an intimate relationship with our writing, it can become just as difficult to lie there as it is in a romantic partnership.

"There's something you're not telling me," a partner will often intuit when we are lying by omission.

Writing says the same thing.

When there is something we are not telling ourselves, our writing points that out. I was not comfortable blaming my friend for having riled me. I was, my writing pointed out, too easily riled. My friend may have been accidentally tactless, but I reacted like I'd sat on a tack. There was something wrong with me and in me that my writing was "right" to point out.

The age of computers and self-publishing brings us to a new and very interesting point. It is now cheap and possible to self-publish. We are no longer so dependent on publishers to shape and disseminate our work. For many years American publishing was dominated by New York and a New York aesthetic. I can remember having novels rejected with a note that read "In New York, this novel feels somehow too romantic and easy. . . ." Of course, I remember thinking, "All of you go to analysts while the rest of the country makes do with trying to love each other!"

Whatever the rest of the country makes do with now, it is a time when regional publishing and small presses—not to mention self-publishing—offer an open door to work that is more personal in nature, perhaps more homespun, often more honest than writing-as-told-to-us by the experts. Just as there is no longer a single aesthetic that tells us what kind of book we "should" be writing, there is now a place to write the kinds of books we want to—books like the one that Kenny and Julia Loggins sent me today.

"Simply put," Loggins wrote me, "this is our love story as told through our journals, love letters, poetry, and lyrics. What reaches the reader through the 'back door' are the teachings of 'conscious relationship.'"

I have been a writer for thirty years and it still excites me when someone decides to claim the full power of writing and write about what they damn well choose as honestly as they possibly can. There is a vigor to such writing, an engaged and emotional timbre that, like Willie Nelson's voice, convinces when something a bit more polished might fail.

The Logginses' book is called *The Unimaginable Life*. It is committed to telling what they call "the total 'unarguable truth.'" For me, it is exciting to read a book like that. It is even more exciting to think, "If they can do it, so can I. So can a lot of us."

It is one of the most frequent fears among would-be writers that they are simply "not original enough." They forget that the root word in "original" is "origin." We are the origin of our work. If that origin is mapped accurately enough, if we are honest enough to

name what we find there, then our work is original. The Logginses'
book is proof of this theorem. I have read more elegant books, but I
have seldom encountered a more readable book, and that, for me, is
where the matter really rests. *The Unimaginable Life* is a brave book. It
pushes the envelope by talking about matters that are personal, private, and so utterly human that they are universal. I found myself responding as I sometimes do to Erica Jong's work: "My God! Now
look what she's saying. I'm so glad somebody is! And I'm glad that it's
her. . . ."

The emotional courage of an artist counts for a lot with me. I can
live with rough edges, with an occasional wince as something cuts
too close to the bone. What I do not want to live with is writing that
is false, slick, or processed like the faux marble that is used to tone up
nouveau riche hotels.

There is something about the truth—like something about a
great plain pine table—that has a beauty and clarity that shine for me
beyond the frequent artifice of High Art.

Am I saying what I mean?

Am I glossing anything over?

Am I giving a pat answer instead of a truthful one?

These are some of the questions we can ask to steer us toward
honesty. Conversely, we can work backward. When our writing feels
mushy, bloated, soft, we can know there is some dishonesty afoot.
Then we can ask:

What truth am I blurring?

What am I afraid to simply say?

What am I unwilling to face?

I recently read a book about "the spiritual journey" which left
me feeling profoundly uncomfortable. It was officially a "spiritual"
book, but there was to the book a competitive, one-up edge that
seemed completely out of place in spiritual matters. There was a cat-
egorizing and calibrating of spiritual experiences that made godliness a
competition, not a compensation for life lived well in a difficult world.

Unlike the Logginses' book—which was full of pettiness but left
me feeling inspired—this book was full of holiness that left me feeling petty. There was something in the writing that I simply did not
trust, a feeling that I was not being told the truth, the whole truth, or

anything like the truth. There was a hollowness to the prose no matter how exalted the topic.

This kind of dissonance, this sound of falseness, is what creeps into our writing when we use it as a place to hide something rather than reveal something. Writing is sheer—like a silk scarf—and the shape of our odd emotional furniture always shows beneath its drapes. This, to my eye, is part of the real reason people have writer's blocks. They do not want to know what they know and so they steer clear of the page and the clarity that it affords us.

"I haven't been writing," my friend Gloria tells me.

"Why not?"

"Ah, well, I'm having trouble with Frankie."

"You thinking of leaving?"

"I don't know. I don't want to know. Probably."

Faced on the page, a difficult truth becomes a doorway. Where we are now becomes the stepping-off point to where we're headed next.

"I've been tracking my pain for three months now. It's getting worse, not better. I'm going to have the cysts removed in December. In January, after I've rested, I'm leaving Frankie."

The truth is not always pleasant, but the results of truth are a solid sense of self, a sane sense of possibility, and a companion to walk us from the life that we've got now into the life we would like better.

For Kenny Loggins and his wife, writing was the bridge from transitory and sad relationships to a deep, grounded, and joyful marriage. Both husband and wife took pen to page with the faith of a farmer tilling a rich but stony field. The work was not easy. The work was not fast, but the work was worth it. "An honest day's work" translated into "an honest day's words." The book they crafted from their life and the life they crafted from their book was "unimaginable" to them when they began.

The writing life may strike you as "unimaginable." It may seem too hard, too daunting, too confrontational. Like the rocky field, it may look like too much work. But the rewards are solid. The gains are real. And on any given day, you need only do an honest day's words and the rest will follow.

H O N E S T Y
Initiation Tool

I call this tool "the Flashlight." Putting things in black and white gives us a flashlight to find our way through the gray. We begin by honestly asking questions. We answer until we arrive at honest answers. The writing itself is the clue to when we are on the right trail. When we are writing honestly, the writing heats up and we can feel that. When we get cold feet about the truth, our prose goes cold as well. Then we need to pry at the icy surface and see what we can dig up. We can try sentences like:

"If I let myself admit it, I . . ."

"If it weren't so risky, I'd . . ."

"If it didn't scare me, I . . ."

"If it weren't so stupid, I'd . . ."

Under the surface, we find our conflicting feelings, the "yes" and "no," the "I love him, but . . ." specificity of emotional honesty. We can trick ourselves by word games into self-disclosure when we are stymied:

What animal is he?

What season is it?

What kind of music?

What food?

Using language, there are a hundred different ways to excavate our buried truths, to arrive at our difficult knowings.

"If it weren't so threatening, I'd admit . . ."

"If I let myself know it, I feel . . ."

"If I let myself feel it, I should . . ."

"If I let myself entertain the thought, I should . . ."

"I'm not ready yet, but eventually I need to . . ."

Any of these gentle prods moves us closer to honesty. When we arrive at internal honesty, internal clarity, it becomes far easier to take external actions. It is a matter of breaking down actions into very small, do-able increments. The page is an ideal place for lists, for brainstorming, for venting and inventing.

VULNERABILITY

You are expensive, Dear. Not like caviar.
Like mistakes in surgery—
An error by the anesthesiologist.
A slip of the knife . . .

THE ABOVE IS A FRAGMENT of an old poem, written to an old lover, about the very real danger I felt he put me in. It is a tough-minded little poem about the softhearted queasy-making vulnerability I was feeling. Writing it out, I stepped back to safety. Writing it out, I experienced my vulnerability and used it to find strength.

Vulnerability in writing is the enemy of grandiosity. It is the enemy of pomposity. It is the enemy of posturing; the enemy of denial. . . . Vulnerability in writing is health, and health—as I can assure you—can be a scary-feeling experience for some of us.

"Why do I feel bad instead of good when I stand up for myself?" my friend Martha sometimes teases me. "Why does getting better feel so much worse?"

Writing well can make us feel temporarily worse because we are breaking the code on ourself. We are shifting patterns we have outgrown. We are shape-shifting into a new form that feels strange to us in its fluidity. We tell ourselves stories about our lives. We believe, "I am this kind of person, not that kind" and then something happens, something jostles us, and we begin, uncomfortably, vulnerably, to wonder, "Maybe I am not so much this sort of person. Maybe I am a little more that sort of person." Pursuing this line of thought, like following the bread crumbs into the forest, brings us to the clearing where the hunters can spot us . . . or brings us to the clearing where the wizard appears.

As we write, we are both describing and deciding the direction that our life is taking. As we become honest on the page about our likes and dislikes, our hopes and dreams, as we become willing to be clear, the murk of our life begins to settle and we see more deeply into our truth. Writing is a practice field. It teaches us how to do happy. It teaches us how to do brave. It teaches us how to do open, caring, loyal, resourceful, and, yes, vulnerable. If we can do it on the page, if we can let our imagination connect the dots, we begin to get a picture of ourselves as larger and more fully human than we may yet have managed.

"But, Julia, shouldn't we write just for the sake of writing? Does it have to be about human improvement?"

Writing doesn't have to be about human improvement, but it can be. Perhaps it simply is.

It is my belief that we are as a species evolving toward something better, not worse, and that writing is one of the primary ways that we are doing it. We are in the midst of a quiet revolution, a revolution of pen and paper.

As more and more of us take to the page, as we explore and express our honest vulnerabilities, first to ourselves and perhaps later for publication, we are rendering ourselves more transparent, more open to the human condition in ourselves and others. We are rendering ourselves compassionate and in that compassion we discover that what we have begun to say, writing, is only the beginning of righting things.

If I put it on the page, it is only a matter of time before I put it into practice. First I observe with more compassion and then I act with more compassion. First I feel my own vulnerability and then I have empathy for the vulnerability of others. The estimable writer Joan Didion has said that writing is the act of saying, "I, I, I." It is, but it is also the act of saying, "He, she, it, they." That, and "we."

Writing centers us in ourselves and it moves us out from that center into the world around us. The "I" of the beholder, the hand that holds the pen, writes to get in touch—and touch is profoundly healing. At its very base, writing may be more about touch than it is about anything else.

We write because something "touches" us. We write because we want to "touch" someone else. We write to "get in touch" with the divine or because the divine has somehow "gotten in touch" with us. When we try to write honestly, we speak of needing to "get in touch with how I really feel." We say, "I'm more in touch with myself."

It would be wonderful if we could write with a surgeon's detachment. It would be comfortable to be clinical and cool as a scalpel. It would also be heartless and, in the end, artless. True art requires true honesty, which means that for our art's sake, as much as for our own, we must learn the skill of vulnerability.

A lot of what frightens people about writing is this precise idea that once we put something on the page we are rendered vulnerable. There is truth to that, but the greater truth, for me, is that once I put something on the page I am also rendered a little less vulnerable. I have created for myself a piece of turf on which I am willing to stand.

This week I have said on the page that I am happy and that I believe I am falling in love. A part of me wants to race ahead in apprehension and say, "Boy. If this doesn't work out, what a jerk you will look like." That's the same part of me that wants to write with one eye on the reviews.

When I think about writing, I remember composer Billy May telling me that we all have a hundred creative horses and that if thirty of our horses are worrying about critics and thirty more are worrying about being too vulnerable, then we have only forty more left to do our work. The trick, Billy May told me, was always to round up your creative horses. In other words, to let ourselves write when we are writing—not worry, fret, stew over how what we write will later be read. This is the conscious practice—the conscious choice—of vulnerability. It is not easy for any of us. It is not easy, but, paradoxically, it is where our strength lies.

I do not like being vulnerable. I do not like feeling exposed and ill at ease. I do not like being stretched beyond my comfort zone—and I do not know how to write or live without trying to find my invulnerability in my vulnerability.

We talk about self-expression but need to pause and remember that self-expression requires a self to express—and that is what we are excavating when we feel our writing has taken us into vulnerable territory.

Vulnerability requires that we contradict ourselves. It requires that we change our minds. It requires that our perspective shifts. Vulnerability, which is honesty's shy younger sister, is the part of ourselves that renders us capable of great art, art that enters and explores the heart.

VULNERABILITY
Initiation Tool

Your writing has by now stirred some of the deeper waters of your soul. Your deeper dreams and desires are more clear to you. The lacks and limitations of your current life stand out in bas relief. This tool asks you to imagine "the unimaginable life." The life that might truly make you happy. It takes courage and vulnerability to admit and imagine our deeper dreams. The irony is that as we are able to envision and clarify for ourselves our deeper dreams, we seem to activate such dreams toward manifestation.

Set aside an hour's private writing time. Set a sacred atmosphere by lighting a candle, perhaps cuing up some expansive music (for me Tim Wheater's flute is an excellent Pied Piper). Set your pen to the page and describe one day in your Ideal Life.

What time do you get up? Where do you live? Whom do you live with? Whom are you working with? What are your hobbies, your pets, your passions?

Allow yourself to dream on the page. Allow yourself to be surprised. Your Ideal Life may be a spiffed-up version of the life you've already got. Your Ideal Life may be radically different, telling you that the time is coming for you to make changes.

Write for forty-five minutes on your Ideal Life. At the end of forty-five minutes, turn your attention back to the life you have right now. Number from one to twenty-five and list twenty-five things you love and appreciate about your life as it is currently constituted.

DAILINESS

It is a bright and lovely day. The sun cleared the mountain before six and lit the field with a calm and even light. We are moving from spring into summer. The days start early, finish late, and stretch long in the middle. The lilacs are finishing. The wild roses are starting. The horses are bored with the winter's hay. I have taken to turning them out for an hour a day and letting them mow what would be a lawn if I were more inclined to niceties.

Just as the season is between summer and spring, I am between my past and my future. I've just finished a novella and a season's teaching and recording. In a few weeks my musical, *Avalon,* will go into rehearsal. Just now? I am structuring my days through writing, and sometimes the writing feels like a bridge across a chasm in a jungle. I am that chasm, that jungle.

I work daily. I get up to write the same way I go out to the barn and toss hay to the horses. It is unthinkable that the horses not be fed and fed in a timely way so they do not get too restless. My creative horses demand the same care. They, too, must be fed and in a timely fashion, and that is why I write first thing in the morning.

For me, writing is nonnegotiable. I do not wait for the right time or the right mood, I simply do it.

"Simply doing it" means that I am sometimes, as now, doing it uphill. It is like exercise. There are days when our body craves it and it is a joy. There are other days when the body resists and each step is a challenge. Again, as with exercise, there is often a shift that happens, a moment when the body crosses from grudging resistance into pleasure in the act of motion.

Writing is the act of motion. Writing is the commitment to move forward, not to stew in our own juices, to become whatever it is that we are becoming. Writing is both the boat and the wind in the sails. Even on the days when the winds of inspiration seem slight, there is some forward motion, some progress made.

Progress, even if that progress is in baby steps, is what writing is about. It is a place of transformation, of spiritual alchemy. We take whatever life has served us and we make something of it. Sometimes it is a simple soup. Sometimes it is a banquet. Sometimes it is a bone to chew on. Always, it is something we can digest.

Daily writing, writing simply for the sake of writing, is like keeping a pot of soup on the back of the stove: it is always there, always ready to be tasted, always ready to be added to, always nourishing, savory, life-sustaining. Like soup, your daily writing doesn't have to be fancy. A few simple ingredients are enough.

Honesty, observation, and imagination are the three ingredients that are the staples. They make up the broth, the basic stock that the rest comes from and adds to. We look at where we are.

I am in a season of soul-shifting. A relationship I have long cherished is falling back from its place at the center of my life. There is space, suddenly, for new beginnings, other loves. I am excited and grieving. The soup I am making today is sweet and sour.

Outside the study window, the light is clear, even, and serene. Birdsong is insistent and repetitive. "Notice me," it says. "I am back." The even light, the spring bird's returning, this time of regret and renewal: that is the broth of what I am making today. Across the field, I notice a black dog, a strange dog, making his way with determined optimism. That dog is onto something. His nose has told him something good is in the offing.

I am not that dog. I am the wary one, waiting to see what a stranger is like before wagging the tail. This has been a long winter. It has been difficult getting by on the stores I had saved. And yet, with a grudging honesty I have to admit that it is spring and my pessimism was a little self-indulgent. Life does intend to be life, abundant and surprising after all.

Which brings me to imagination. If I let myself imagine it, what might I yet be able to do that I would enjoy? If I relinquish the shape of life as I had known it, life with its known elements, its wintry stock of goods, if I recognize that the blossoms outside my window are the promise of fruit, what then?

This is the question daily writing always asks, "What then?"

Here is where I am and how I feel. (Observation and honesty.) Here is what I can do with that. (Imagination.) In other words, daily writing is both the room you are living in and the doorway to the world just beyond. Walking across the room of your experience a word at a time, you reach the doorway, and, even if you are a prisoner of your current circumstances, you can swing that door open in your mind. Sometimes the hinges will groan. Sometimes the door will sigh with relief. Sometimes opening the door will bring in so much light and clarity that—quick!—you will slam it shut. Writing lets you do all that and watch all that. Writing holds up a mirror, offers a harmony, holds out a companionable hand. Writing says wherever you are is meaningful and the beginning of being somewhere else.

In this sense, writing is the meditative act of cherishing. It is a pathway into ourselves and into our Self. If we witness our own lives and our own thoughts with accuracy, taking it down as we see and hear it, we find ourselves witnessing something larger than we had realized at first. We find ourselves witnessing life. We find ourselves learning.

It is my belief that any regular practice is a good practice. It is my belief that if you bicycle, it will teach you. If you walk, it will teach you. If you bake bread or write poems, it will teach you. What will teach you is the "it" that you do because that "it" is doing you: doing you a favor, doing you a service, doing you a good turn, a grace, a job.

As practices go, writing is a handy practice in every sense: it is done by hand, done easily, done without much rigmarole or fuss. It is a democratic practice. We can all do it. There is no need for a special diet, for a special room, for special shoes or even a special time. All that is required is that we show up on the page.

The ability to show up brings with it the ability to grow up. (We talk a great deal about the fact that creativity involves the nurturance

of our inner child, but it also involves the participation and apprecia-
tion of our inner adult!)

The willingness to face the page brings with it the willingness to
face the music. Sometimes that music is a heart-cradling waltz. Sometimes that music is modern and discordant. Whatever the music is, it
is what we are dancing to that day. Although we may not pause to acknowledge it, there is a rhythm that runs through our days, and that
rhythm can be chaotic or steady, choppy or soothing, strident or
smooth. By consciously listening to our daily music, we put ourselves
in harmony with reality.

Reality happens in daily doses. Life lived a day at a time is life
made much of. It is not that we cannot see the larger picture or that
we do not need to acknowledge the larger movements in our life, but
movements in life, as in a symphony, are made from myriad tiny
notes, each one a point of consciousness.

Writing to ourselves, we are taking note as to the notes we are
playing. We are hearing ourselves as we sing our song. We are able,
then, to be instrumental in our own change. We become not merely
players but conductors/composers as well.

As I write this book—feeding the horses, the dogs, and the wild
songbirds, feeding myself a steady diet of daily writing—I find myself
coming to the kind of clarity that can rise up only out of a steady practice. Earlier this week my writing pointed out that I was in self-pity.
"Ah-ha," I thought, "too many strings." I needed the pizzicato of
some crisp, businesslike actions. I needed to put in more stings and
fewer strings.

Writing may express the self, but it also quiets the self. It siphons
off the busy chatter of distraction and points a way to hear the larger
currents moving more deeply in ourselves. In other words, writing allows both the small and the large to have their place.

Spring in Taos Valley: the Sacred Mountain is dripping with fragrant clouds. The lilacs are lush and heavy. The sagebrush pushes perfume into the night wind like an expensive woman getting on an
elevator. There is no escaping the sensuality of where I am living.
The spring will turn to summer. Summer will burn into fall. The sage
will grow dry, then go silver. Winter will come again. Writing, it is all
good. It is all happiness, just different forms and colors and shades of

happiness than might at first be selected. Writing gives me the chance to see past my first perceptions, through my idealizations and my wishes to what may be more solid, more enduring, more lastingly joyful than I at first perceived.

Outside my study window, two delicate finches are nibbling at the feeder. The clear morning sun has given way to a silvery overcast. The horses are busy deconstructing the north pasture fence and the wild roses along my courtyard wall are opening their gold and crimson hearts. The birdsong encircling the house is sibilant and various. The UPS truck has just pulled up outside. In all of these particulars, the fact that shines forward for me is that in writing about my life I cherish it. I value it. I see it. Writing is the act of opening the eye to the absolute beauty of ordinary things. That is dailiness and dailiness is sanity.

DAILINESS
Initiation Tool

This tool requires ten minutes daily for one consecutive week. The minutes are to be those just before sleep. Take pen in hand and gently review your day in a few simple sentences: "Today was productive but uphill. I seemed to be fighting a depression but I took good actions anyhow. I'm really stewing over my friendship with Michael. I wonder what better can be done on the project at work. . . ." Out of your writing, try to distill a single question to pose to your unconscious and sleep on. For example, "What should I do about Michael?" or "What can I do about the project at work?" Simply pose the question on the page. Do not worry about answering. You may find—using this evening process—that answers emerge for you in your next Morning Pages.

Be alert, in the use of this tool, to notice and tabulate small, positive changes. "I got out for a walk. I got my sister called back. The meeting at work went well." If Morning Pages help set the tone and pace of the days we have, Evening Notes help in cherishing the blessings such dailiness has to offer.

VOICE

A GREAT DEAL OF attention is paid in critical circles to the concept of having "a voice" in writing. It is my belief that all of us have a voice in writing because all of us have a voice. Working to have a "unique" voice is another concept that gets a great deal of play. I believe that each of us already has a unique voice. We do not need to "develop" it; rather, we need to discover or, perhaps better, uncover it.

This may sound like semantic quibbling, but to my eye it is not. The minute we start thinking of writing as something exalted and difficult, the minute we begin to imagine we must construct something—"a voice"—in order to be able to do it, writing becomes an elusive and difficult art rather than a birthright—or a birth-write.

When we focus on having a voice to the exclusion of having something to say, we put the cart before the horse. If we allow ourselves to enter into what we want to express, we will intuitively arrive at appropriate ways to express it.

Go back for a minute to the physical voice that we are all born with. That voice rests on a foundation. That foundation is the breath. When a singing teacher seeks to open a voice, the foundation step is proper breathing: regular, repetitive, and from the gut.

There is no better way to open a writing voice than to write regularly, repetitively, and from the gut. I write Morning Pages every day.

They are like doing scales. They take me up and down my emotions, up and down my life circumstances, up and down my actions and reactions—and they take about twenty minutes.

For about two decades now I have been teaching creative unblocking and, occasionally, creative writing. In both cases, I ask students to lay a foundation of regular, repetitive writing from the gut. This is their writer's breath work. This is the foundation on which all else rests.

"But, Julia, I have a novel to write."

"Learn to write regularly and easily and you will write the novel regularly and easily."

For the past years I have worked with composer Tim Wheater. I have been learning to sing and Wheater has been helping me to do it. He has taught me to make simple tones—single vowels, the sonic equivalent of small one-syllable words—and then string those tones together. This is called "toning."

"What does toning have to do with singing?" I want to say, the same way my students wonder what regular morning writing has to do with novels, plays, and films.

"If you tone well, you sing well. Singing is really just toning on a more complex level," Mr. Wheater tells me.

"Ah."

If singing is toning on a more complex level and yields you a beautiful voice, so, too, writing regularly and repetitively and from the gut yields you a writing voice that is full and beautiful regardless of which genre you apply it in.

"But, Julia, don't you have to be original to have a voice?"

"You are original. You are the origin of your work."

Writing from the body—dropping down into the well of your experience and sounding out how you feel—ultimately yields a body of work. We say that a voice is full-bodied without realizing that this is a literal phrase: when we write from our gut rather than from our head we acquire the same resonance that a singer does when the breath comes from the diaphragm rather than high up in the chest.

What do I mean by "writing from the gut"?

We talk about a "gut reaction." We mean by that the instantaneous knowing that seems to skip the usual circuitry of the mind.

Writing can be done the same way. It can be done by listening to how we feel rather than thinking about how we feel. Writing from the gut is largely a matter of evading the censor. For most of us the censor changes size on a daily basis. It's like Alice in Wonderland: some days the censor is huge, omnivorous, hard to get around; other days, the censor is smaller, a grating little voice of disapproval. The trick is to both miniaturize the censor and to accept the censor—and to write despite what the censor has to say.

For myself, I often think of the censor as an annoyingly negative relative, the wet blanket at the party. Because there is no way to do Morning Pages wrong—they are simply three daily Morning Pages of anything—this writing trains the censor to back off and trains us, as writers, to work despite the censor's presence. In other words, Morning Pages are one way of learning to write from the gut.

I have several other tricks that I use. I will take a telling phrase like "What I'd really like to say is _____" and then I'll finish it twenty times. Sometimes I'll choose "What I'm scared to say is _____." Sometimes I will use "What it would really be fun to say is _____."

Right now, for example, my gut is telling me that anyone reading this already knows and has had the experience of writing from the gut. It's the straight-from-the-hip writing we do when we write to someone we know "gets us." That's when we put in all the little hooks and crooks that we censor from less friendly eyes. In other words, finding our voice has to do with finding our safety. This is what Frank Miriam, Sinéad O'Connor's singing teacher, teaches as "letting the song do the singing." His belief, as mine, is that if you concentrate on what you are saying, the how will take care of itself.

When we become too complicated, too self-conscious and topiary in our prose, not only our literary voice but our soul itself seems to suffer. "Sell your cleverness and buy bewilderment," the poet and mystic Rumi advised.

The best advice I was ever given about writing came to me early in my writing career from Arthur Kretchmer, the editor of *Playboy*.

"Don't bother to write for your common reader, Julia," Arthur told me. "You'll never meet your common reader. Write for your ideal reader, the one who will get everything you say."

In other words, the reader who makes you feel safe.

Right now, my ideal reader is David. Last night after talking to him on the phone, I quickly wrote:

SAFETY

This is what safety feels like.
It is a very large room.
It is light and airy.
There is a fire, a reading chair,
A window with a view.
This is what safety feels like.
And it's you.

This morning I am happy and excited. My bird feeders have attracted a squadron of great birds. The house is filled with birdsong. The wild roses are glorious, a splendid consolation for the lilacs leaving for another year. This book, the one I have found alternately difficult and exhilarating to write, is, in fact, writing itself. It reminds me that while I may hope to have a voice, my real business is to give voice, to allow what is trying to be written to write through me.

When we become willing to be an empty vessel, we must let go of ideas of how our work should look and should sound. It is the same problem for writers as it is for actors. If an actor has an "idea" of the performance he is trying to give, that concept gets in the way of being true to the moment-to-moment life that is trying to move through him. Similarly, as writers, if we spend too much time conceptualizing our work rather than actualizing it, we become stuck in how something should look and that leaves us caught on a surface level when the work itself may wish to move deeper. (This is why "high concept" films are often so frustrating. Their concept overpowers any subtlety in what they are saying.)

In writing—as in acting, singing, dance, any of the arts—perfection is found not in control but in surrendering to the control of the art itself. A dancer will say, "Dance dances through me." A painter will say, "The painting paints through me." Paradoxically we work to control a medium until we have enough control to allow the medium to control us.

The long practice of daily work gives us the muscles and sinews to uphold the work that wants to move through us. The dancer's leg is trained not to quaver. So, too, we are trained as writers not to waver in the act of listening. By listening to what it is we are meant to write on a daily basis, we learn to let our writing write through us.

A writing voice is not a collection of ticks and tricks. A writing voice is a vehicle for communication. The individuality of a voice emerges not by falling in love with your own facility but by learning to move past it.

Too much cleverness gets in the way of real writing and real thought. A writer who falls in love with his own writing voice is like Narcissus leaning too far over the pond in love with his own reflection. Thought and voice turned in upon themselves become stagnant and decadent. Writing that is too "heady" cuts us off from the heart. This is the problem addressed in the following poem, a poem about the problem of cleverness.

ABBA, FATHER

I have made myself a word I can't pronounce.
I've made an alphabet of choices
Made from voices not my own.
Dancing cheek to cheek,
My Chinese with my Greek,
Geography, cartography—
Calligraphy is left to me.
The nub of it is this:
My syllables all hiss a name I cannot say.
I strike me mute.
I kick me like a boot.
I want the simple truth
To speak my name.
Abba, Father, come to me like water.

Wet my tongue,
And teach me what I've sung.

The Lakota Indians believe that each of us has a life song. I believe this too. It is my experience born out in many years of teaching. People who begin writing thinking that they have nothing to say move into their writing and discover that they have a world to say and that that world needs them to say it.

Not long ago I was cornered by a crusty writer who demanded to know when I was going to stop this business of convincing people to write.

"I'm not going to," I told him.

"But think of all the bad writers you may be making!"

"That's not my experience."

"Oh. You mean some of these new writers are actually good?" the writer sneered defensively.

"Lots of them are actually good. Some of them are actually exquisite. It's a profoundly humbling experience for me to realize that I may be midwiving talents into the world who are far more gifted than some of us who have made quite a stir."

"Mmm." Displeased with what I'd told him, the writer drifted off.

My experience as a teacher tells me that it is never too late for someone to find their writing voice. Students of mine who began writing in their mid-fifties have gone on to win playwrighting contests and poetry festivals. A woman who took pen to paper at seventy is publishing her first novel. All too often what is missing in a voice is only confidence.

Dear Julia,
    You convinced me to start writing and even though I thought you were crazy, I did it. Enclosed find the children's book I have just published. . . .

Sometimes we do not know we have a writing voice because there has never been anyone to listen. When we begin to listen ourselves, the inner voice grows stronger. Soon others can hear it as well and a circle of support can start to grow.

Dear Julia,

After thirty years of teaching, I have finally found my own voice. I love writing! I only wish I hadn't waited so long. Please tell your other students to trust you and begin where they are.

Yes: Dear Other Students. Trust me and begin where you are!

VOICE
Initiation Tool

When we are less than well physically, we sometimes "lose" our voice. In truth, we haven't lost it. We have lost the use of it. When we are psychologically unwell, we often "lose" our inner voice. Again, what we have lost is really the use of it. The Inner Voice is still there, waiting to be rediscovered and reconnected to.

For this tool you are asked to time-travel back along your own life—your narrative time line—and stop at a time or an episode that is emotionally charged for you. You are then asked to scoop this "cup" of time from your life and write about it.

The term "cup" comes from a gold-mining tool, the "cupel," which is used to sift the gold ore from the dross. This is the same function that writing a cup has for a writer. When we write about something we care about, something in which we have an emotional stake, our writing automatically acquires "voice." Of course it does. We are speaking of emotional truth. A few examples of possible cups are:

1. My family had a secret.
2. My favorite relative
3. My near death experience
4. My greatest loss
5. My greatest win
6. My parents' marriage

7.   My closest friend
8.   My closest call
9.   My worst betrayal
10. My happiest memory

As a general rule, cups range from several up to ten typed pages. As you write, you will experience a sense of shape and length within the material itself. Very often a short, densely packed cup becomes the seed for a later and larger piece of work.

When you have finished your cup, you may wish to share it with what I call a "friendly reader." By definition a friendly reader is someone who loves writing and is able to read for the sheer joy of reading and not to play armchair critic. It is wise to explain to your friendly reader that you are embarking on a series of such cups and that you have been told to ask for positive feedback on what works well in the writing. In this way, you will learn to build on your writing strength rather than focus on and magnify your writing weaknesses. Many students mail their cups off to some of the people involved. Recipients often report being deeply touched by these written memoirs.

A final word of caution: be careful not to share your cups with critical readers, blocked writers, or those for whom the material of the cups is an inflammable emotional issue. The point of sharing cups is to garner support, not controversy. Some students find it best to share cups in an open mike setting rather than entrust a single reader or divulge the cups to the parties also involved. Use your own good judgment as to when, where, and how you share your cup. It is the first of many.

FORM VERSUS FORMULA

I AM WRITING THIS ESSAY in an edit suite for ABC's *In Concert*. It is a gray electronic bunker where next weekend's viewing is being shaped amid Coke cans, Marlboro lights, and the steady punch, punch, punch of buttons, choices, options.

In my years as a filmmaker, editing became my favorite process. I loved choice, choice, choice. I loved options, variables, the emergence of polish. As a writer, I love both the act of initial writing—laying track—and the act of editing or rewriting, but I carefully divide them into two separate processes.

"Scrutinize second," I laid down a rule for myself. "Write first and freely."

Once I became willing to stand aside, a literate force seemed to write through me.

"Would you call it channeling? Did you channel *The Artist's Way*?" I am sometimes asked.

I didn't call it channeling. I didn't call it anything but a blessed relief—and, perhaps, "listening."

First drafts became like listening to an old forties radio show. I wrote in installments, clicking the set to "on" when I settled in to write. When I finished, I clicked the set to "off." I began to trust that just like a radio, I could turn "it," writing, on again tomorrow.

No longer struggling to be brilliant, I aimed, instead, at being attentive. I listened for the thread of what it was I was hearing—or writing. I listened and wrote down what I heard.

Very often, I found in my rewrites, I had all the right elements, just slightly out of order. A simple reshuffling of paragraphs often gave me all the polish I needed. It was easy to reshuffle when all the elements were there—it was much easier than trying to get the elements right the first time out. Rewriting became a matter of re-righting, of putting things in place rather than reinventing the wheel.

"The wheel," in fact, is a useful term: if first-draft writing is a matter of simply laying track, then rewriting becomes a matter of traveling that track in a handcart, the old-fashioned pump kind you see in old movies. Wheeling along in the handcart, you can see where the joints are missing, where the transitions need to be laid. You look for and fix potential trouble spots before the fully laden locomotive of your readership comes along. Viewed this way, writing and rewriting are two separate but logical processes.

I am writing now in the sound booth at a U2 concert. ABC's *In Concert* is filming it. The stage is a football field away. Around me, video decks and tape decks buzz and whir. There is a wall of monitors, a bank of mixing switches, and a small army of sound technicians in de rigueur blue jeans and black T-shirts on countdown to get sound and image right.

Onstage, a hundred-foot golden arch, a sixty-foot lemon, an olive skewered on a swizzle stick are the paraphernalia of "pop." This tour is "Popmart"—a commentary on the pop of culture and the culture of pop.

The air is electric—quite literally—but also filled with energy and enthusiasm. The army of techies dance in their places while I sit quietly amid the mayhem, jotting notes. If writing is about listening, it is also about seeing and getting on the page exactly what you see and hear.

So often, for so many of us as writers, it is the failure of faith in the moment that leaches our writing of power. This book, for example, began at 7,500 feet in the Sangre de Cristo mountains during a lush and redolent spring. The mood of that spring was deeply romantic. If this book were being shaped instead of shaping itself, this rock and roll concert would be off limits no matter what lessons it had to teach. What, after all, does ABC's *In Concert* have to do with writing?

A great deal, it seems to me—at least with the kind of writing I like: live, sweaty, juiced up, uncensored. There is a purity to live performance, a magic to the roughness of the moment that is true for predominantly first-draft writing as well. Rewrites are fine—like studio work is fine—but the high-wire act of live performance, like the high-wire act of writing from the heart, the gut, and the seat of the pants, yields work with energy, passion, and drive. Just as there is a democracy inherent in rock and roll—we all feel the beat—there is a propulsive power in the written word when it is written and not overly rewritten. This joie de vivre, this kick-in-the-pants power, comes when we allow form to triumph over formula. In other words, when we trust that writing "live" has a real and valid life to it.

"But, Julia," I am often asked, "what about shape, form, structure?"

"What you are writing has a shape, has a form, has a structure," I reply. "Your job is to discover it, not improve it. The writing knows what to write."

"How do you know the writing knows? How can you have such faith?"

I don't have faith alone. I have experience—lots and lots of writing experience. It is not theory to me that the writing knows what needs to be written. It is experience, long, deep, experience. It is not only that I have over and over experienced the inner wisdom of a piece of writing, it is also that I have had my own failures of faith, the times where I have wasted time and energy fighting with a piece of work when my intellectual idea of what I wanted it to do differed from the organic form that was wisely unfolding. We call what we write "brainchildren," and just as a pregnancy must not be overstressed and artificially hurried for fear of damaging or aborting the child, so, too, a piece of work asks that we not try to force it in unnatural directions.

In the edit suite at ABC, back at this essay's beginning, I listened while David worked on a show. He reshaped the acts, editing out one group altogether.

"But we planned!" the editor protested.

"Not in this show," David said firmly. The "plan" was one thing. The show's own organic plan was another. The show had its own inherent shape, and what looked good on paper didn't hold up on the screen.

"Shoot it. You can always cut it" is a filmmaking motto, the filmmaking equivalent of laying first-draft track.

"Write it, you can always change it," I amend the motto to apply to all writing. This is the rule of thumb for first drafts. This is the starting gate. There is glee in the purity of simply laying track. It's live performance and it's real. After that? It's the editing room: choice, choice, choice. There is glee, too, in the discernment of editing. By keeping the two processes separate, as they are in film, each process brings a pure, untrammeled joy. They work together, one might say, "in concert."

FORM VERSUS FORMULA
Initiation Tool

Very often what stands between us and our writing is a desire to be able to write perfectly, to spare ourselves rough drafts and even rough spots. We want to be able to perfectly conceive a final product and write that. This desire to avoid what we think of as dead ends often keeps us from writing. In order to write freely, we must be willing to write less formally. We must allow our writing to be a process that helps us to process.

Take yourself "out" to write. Settle into your writing spot, get comfortable, and number from one to five. Now list five circumstances in which you could use your writing. For example:

1. I could write Dad.
2. I could do a memo about the new project.
3. I could write my college roommate.
4. I could write my congressperson on a special issue.
5. I could write another cup.

Select one from the five topics and start writing. Allow yourself enough time to rough out an entire draft of what you want to say. Allow yourself to enter your body and experience the feeling of your hand, writing. Let yourself enjoy the feeling of a piece of work coming to form through you.

When you have finished writing, take a moment to reflect on how much more freely you are now able to write. If you've written a letter, you may want to post it. If you've roughed out a memo or more formal letter, you may want to put it into typed form. If your choice was to write another cup, you may want once again to find a suitable venue in which to share it. A reader is part of the writer's life cycle.

FOOTWORK

I'M AT MY WIT'S END."

The voice on the phone belonged to a woman writer.

"Why are you are your wit's end?"

"Oh, I've been working on this project forever and there's no pleasing this editor and so now I am stalling."

"Stalling?"

"It practically takes a gun to get me to the page."

"How are you managing?"

"I tell myself, 'Just write it. Inevitably this editor will want changes and you can make changes later. For now, just do the best you can.'"

"Why not do the best you can and do some footwork?"

"What do you mean 'footwork'?"

"Is this the only editor in the world?"

"Oh. I couldn't do that."

"Why not?"

"Well, it doesn't seem very loyal."

"Your first loyalty needs to be to you and to your work."

"I'll think about it."

"Meanwhile, do the best you can."

There are many times in a writing life when "just doing the best you can" requires separating the act of writing from its eventual reception. This is a difficult bit of mental maneuvering and one where we sometimes need to call in our spiritual resources. Sometimes, we need prayers to just finish the blasted project. Sometimes, we have to pretend to ourselves that the only eyes that will ever see a manuscript are our own. Other times, we may need to enlist the help of a "Friendly Reader" so that at least one person will see and enjoy a manuscript before it gets picked to pieces. Sometimes, our resistance toward working in a certain situation means that we need to do the footwork to enable us to work somewhere else.

Carolyn, a gifted and prolific magazine writer, had enjoyed a two-year stint of loving what she wrote and having her editor at a major woman's magazine love what she wrote as well. All of that changed when her editor left the magazine and another editor was assigned in her place. This editor was actually a blocked writer. She felt competitive toward Carolyn although she couldn't admit those feelings directly. Furthermore, she had ideas on how she herself would write each of Carolyn's assignments and so, rather than receive Carolyn's work with an open mind, she received each article as a failed attempt to hit an invisible target.

"For a long time, I did not understand what was going on," Carolyn told me. "I kept thinking, 'She's a writer. She should understand.' I did not think, 'She's a blocked writer and she resents my getting a byline.'"

It was Carolyn's therapist who suggested the possibility of competition to Carolyn. Although it caught her by surprise, Carolyn saw instinctively that the diagnosis fit.

"I saw that I had to put a two-pronged plan into action. First of all, I had to find a way to keep writing for this editor. Secondly, I had to find other editors for whom I could work."

In order to keep writing for the competitive editor, Carolyn had to free herself from defensive perfectionism. She had to "just write it" and know that whatever she wrote would inevitably have to be rewritten. There was no "doing it right" because there was no "right." Once she accepted that, Carolyn felt free to write more easily and began to treat her redrafts as a place where she and the editor could work together creatively.

Meanwhile, Carolyn xeroxed her best clips, put together a query letter, and sent it out to other editors at magazines in her field. To her surprise, the queries met with immediate interest.

"We've long talked about the fact that we wanted someone like you writing for us," one editor phoned her to say.

Without burning her bridges at magazine A, Carolyn accepted two assignments from magazines B and C. She thought of this as an experiment in open-mindedness—and an attack on her own inertia.

"I found one new editor whom I really liked and one editor even worse than the one I was dealing with. I felt like I got a reality check on the actual 'lay of the land' in my field and I felt less cornered and victimized."

Galvanized by the pain of her work situation into taking action in her own behalf, Carolyn arrived at a basic fact that is often under-discussed and overlooked: publishers need writers to publish. Without willing writers, publishers cannot flourish. As much as a publisher might want to act like a writer is dispensable, they actually do need us. Just as publishers so ominously warn writers, they, too, "can be replaced."

"I've decided you're right and I need to do some footwork."

It was my friend the frustrated writer again.

"What made you decide that?"

"I was going through too many gymnastics emotionally. I was having to pretend I was never going to turn a piece in, that I was really writing for someone else, that I wasn't getting demoralized when in fact what I was feeling was a murderous rage."

"Well, a murderous rage is probably better than a suicidal depression."

"Oh, I felt that too. But I decided I thought you were right about loyalty."

"What about loyalty?"

"That I needed to be loyal to myself."

It is a spiritual maxim that God never closes one door without opening another. It is a spiritual joke that while this may be true, the hallway in between is murder. When we are "stuck" in our writing lives, it is usually because we are clinging to a situation that has outlived its usefulness to us or we are unwilling to explore a new risk that we sense that we really must take.

Carter, a nonfiction writer, felt himself pigeonholed as a writer who wrote stories about only his specialty. He could not get his editor to assign him work outside his tried and true area. And yet, he balked at writing an article just on speculation, telling himself he was "beyond all that." Feeling underappreciated and trapped, Carter found himself mired in resentment and depression. His wife finally took him to task.

"I married you because you were a writer who loved his work and whose work I loved. Now you are a writer who hates his work. I think you need to go back to writing what you want whether anybody is paying you to do that or not. At least that way, you'll respect yourself."

Prompted by his wife's remarks, Carter allowed himself to move out on spec into the area he was interested in.

"I felt like a real writer again once I was writing about what I wanted to and—here's the irony—the very editor who wouldn't assign me a piece outside my specialty is the editor who bought the piece that I wrote on spec. Sometimes I think we just have to prove to the world that we take ourselves seriously in order for others to jump on the bandwagon."

"I realized I was like a skier," Carter told me. "Every once in a while as a writer, I just need a good, long downhill run. This means that sometimes I need to write without thinking about an editor, without thinking about where it will get published. I need to write something just for the joy of writing it."

Whether you call it "doing the footwork" or "taking yourself seriously," what is actually required at many points in a writing career is the grace to allow ourselves to one more time be a beginner writing for the sheer love of it.

FOOTWORK
Initiation Tool

The dreadful thing about doing footwork is that it insists that we take responsibility. Who wants to do that? And alone and unaided? Most of us need a sense of support when we are contemplating moving out into concrete risks. This tool asks that you actively seek a sense of spiritual support.

You are asked to take a notepad, get out of the house, and take yourself to a sacred place. For some this is a church or synagogue. For others it is a library, a park, a cliff overlooking the ocean. Settle into your sacred space, take pen in hand, ask for inspiration, and then brainstorm. Fill in the following sentences:

1. It would be a support to my writing life if I let myself:

    1.

    2.

    3.

    4.

    5.

2. I would feel better about my writing life if I tried:

    1.

    2.

    3.

    4.

    5.

After filling out these brainstorming questions, take five more minutes to acknowledge yourself and go back over five ways in which you have already helped your writing life to prosper. Fill in the following:

I have helped myself to have a writing life by:

1.
2.
3.
4.
5.

PRACTICE

I AM WRITING IN A TONY espresso shop on Park Avenue. Outside, it's a sunny, hot June day. The avenue is noisy and full of rush-hour irritation. The espresso shop is a cool, dark cave.

Wherever I am, whenever I can, I write. I put my hand to the page and my thoughts to the test. Am I balanced? Overreacting? Happy? Sad? My hand moving across the page teaches me my emotional weather. It tracks my moods, my progress, the places where I am "out of reality." It grounds me into specifics, into cause and effect, into perspective.

Just as the espresso shop is a retreat from the city—"It was once a church," my friend Gerard tells me—the page is a cool cave of consciousness, somewhere to both meditate on life and savor it. In Buddhist terms, my writing is a "practice."

Practice means what it says: writing is something to be done over and over, something that improves through the repetitive doing but that needs not be done perfectly. Just as a piano teacher will tell you to practice scales, that consistency is the key to mastering the instrument, as a writing teacher I have said the same thing. Consistency is the key to mastering the instrument that is you.

You, the writer, are a spiritual instrument. If you allow yourself to write consistently, you will become more and more finely tuned. You will become more and more fluid and expressive. As you become more fluid and expressive, you will become more vibrant, more vital, more alive.

While our mythology tells us that writing is about the ivory tower, writing itself teaches an interest in life outside the tower. The artist is not a prisoner of art locked in the prison of the self. No! Art sets the artist free. Art is the key to freedom. Art is the doorway to a larger, livelier, and more involved self. I have said "an involved self" and not "self-involved." The consistent practice of art is a bridge between the self and the world.

The nave of the espresso shop has a black marble floor mottled with green. Display cases host gelatos, Italian ices, pastries of many stripes. The small tables are green faux marble. The rear wall is mirrored and reflects the shiny silver espresso machine, the snowy stacks of white cups, saucers, and dessert plates. 106.7 FM is playing easy to listen to oldies but goldies. I find myself thinking about married friends of mine, Daniel and Lucinda, two actor-writers. I think of the consistent passion they bring to their life together, their insistence on being consistently present to the flow between them moment to moment. Writing, I think, is just such an intimate relationship. It requires commitment—a thankless word, but perhaps a more accurate one than "discipline," the word always used.

I've been writing full-time for thirty years. I am sure there are some people who would say I am married to my work, but that is not how I experience it. I experience writing as a love affair, one I am free to leave but choose to enjoy. It is intimate. It is daily. It is year in and year out, but, oh, it is romantic. It is free. It is passionate—like a long and intricate conversation with a fascinating man.

There is a tension, an excitement, a spark of possibility in all great conversation. If writing is a conversation with life, then we must bring to that conversation our alert attention, our willingness to be surprised. We must bring to our writer's world an open eye, an eye that is focused on the world around us and not merely on the inner world of our own concerns.

Writing rewards practice. Writing rewards attention. Writing, like sex with the right partner, remains a gateway to greater mystery, a way to touch something greater than ourself. Writing is an act of cherishing. It is an act of love: I love this and this and this. Like any great love, writing is specific—not generic. If we are to write well, we must practice being specific.

Rush hour is thinning. Evening strollers are intermingled with homebound workers. Pet owners, home from work, begin the evening ritual of walking their pets. A sense of emotionality and devotion interjects itself onto the street. Love, that constant and elusive variable, makes itself felt in the bond between dog and owner, the linked hand-in-hand intimacy of lovers reunited, joining each other after their office days for an early meal, a quick movie. Asphalt notwithstanding, tenderness is afoot. The evening sky softens its light. It is a beautiful night.

Behind the counter, the waitress foams a cappuccino, arranges a plate of petits fours. She has black curly hair, a white blouse, a full figure. She is the luscious bride from *Il Postino,* a classical figure of femininity. Watching her, writing her, I am connected to the flow of life. A passing mother with a small, dark-haired daughter enters the shop with their chow dog, Cinnamon. It's a little visit to Caesar, the shop's owner.

In the deepest corner, an older woman with a girlish Veronica Lake hairdo sips an iced coffee and marks the transition from day to evening with a slice of homemade pizza. Now the *Godfather* theme wafts through the shop with haunting plangency. Caesar greets a new patron by offering a watermelon soda. An elderly woman enters with a small, spotted dog.

Observed closely enough, all of life is interesting. The practice of writing teaches this. All of life is filled with drama. Observed closely, small moments have large impact. They are like the small variations as we move scale to scale in piano practice. The eye, like the ear, becomes trained to nuance by consistent attention. Just as Bach's "Goldberg Variations" charmed an insomniac prince, our focused attention charms the part of ourselves that is restive and disordered. When we practice the art of close observation, we gain an emotional palette that has more shades, more possibilities, than the screaming extremes of black and white headlines declaring catastrophe and crisis.

"Look at the top of that apartment building," Gerard will direct as we walk. "It's a Stanford White building. It used to be the home of Gorham silver." Always pointing out some detail, some nuance of architecture or light, Gerard is an appreciator—a warmer word than connoisseur—of his city. Seeing Manhattan through his eyes, I am constantly delighted, caught by fresh and exciting detail. Gerard teaches English literature, and he has a writer's voracious eye.

To practice writing consistently is to be caught by detail, to be snagged by delight. The beautiful waitress pours fresh water. Caesar fusses with the espresso machine. Carmine Coppola's melodies swell and ebb as deliciously as the steam and foam of the great silver machine. Evening falls.

Everything I have written about happens daily, the same but differently. Writing it out, it is impossible not to love, not to cherish, not to connect to it. If writing is a practice, it is also perfect.

PRACTICE
Initiation Tool

Very often we live without consciousness of what it is we are actually doing and how it is we spend our time. We listen to the voice-over in our head that says, "I'll get to it tomorrow," rather than observe just how it is we spend today. This tool asks you to "watch the picture without the sound," that is, to observe your day as if you were shooting silent footage for a documentary film. This observation will tell you what you think you practice and what you actually do practice.

Set aside a quiet and private hour. Light a candle, some incense if you choose. Put your hand to the page and describe—in clear detail—a day in your life as you currently lead it. Describe yourself as the character who owns this life.

What do you look like? What choices do you make? What wishes do you, as a character, harbor? What are the loves in the life you lead? Do you listen to hot jazz, walk a sunny fox terrier, specialize in wok cookery? If you were a novel, who would have written you? For that matter, what do you regularly read? Write for a full forty-five minutes, describing yourself as if you were a fictional character. At the end of forty-five minutes, stop.

What did you learn? Write for fifteen minutes about the insights you have garnered by viewing yourself as a character.

CONTAINMENT

O<small>N A RECENT</small> teaching trip to Ireland, I met a talented young Scots writer. He was just in the process of finding his feet on the page. He was brimming with words, energy, and enthusiasm. He had the ripe, ready-to-write energy that I have come to recognize in myself and others. I was excited for the future I was sure he would have.

"Please write," I told him. Fax numbers were exchanged.

Back from the trip, I got two excellent short stories written and faxed within a week. Just as I'd hoped, the writing was excellent—sound and surefooted. This young man was a real find, a gold mine of creative energy. All he had to do was let himself use it.

"Great stories," I shot back. "Keep it up."

I anticipated a flow of stories. It was exciting to watch a young writer finding his voice. I couldn't wait to hear more of it—but I didn't. Instead, there was fax silence, and then . . .

"I showed my stories to my friends. They didn't think much of them. They said they didn't get them," the young writer reported brokenly. "I haven't had any other story ideas since."

I wanted to get on an airplane, go back to Ireland, and commit my own terrorist acts. How dare these supposed "friends" criticize work that was so strong and vigorous and promising? Who did they think they were . . . critics?

The best and rarest criticism is constructive, and very few people know how to give it. This being the case, the wisest thing to do with early writing—and early drafts of all writing—is to practice the art of containment.

"You must practice containment," I told the young writer. "Stop showing your stories around, especially to your friends. Just write more of them and send them over by fax. Let's aim for an even dozen. Write first. Worry about fixing them later."

All this young writer needs to find his stride—all any of us needs, really—is encouragement and safety. This does not mean that aesthetics go out the window. It means, however, that we need to take the time and the space to discover our own aesthetic, and that does not happen when we get involved with instant cup of soup criticism and art by consensus. The question "What do you think of my writing?" must always be superseded by the real question, "What do I think of my writing?"

Once upon a time we talked about "the love of letters." We don't do this much anymore. I wish we would go back to talking about the love of letters and writing from the love of letters and, perhaps, to writing love letters. At its base, for me, love is what writing is about. As an act of love, it deserves our protection and our deepest respect.

Medieval cities flourished within high walls that guarded their perimeters. Each of us contains a creative core that must be protected in precisely the same way. I think of my creativity as my most valuable asset. It is my wealth. I know that, and I protect that in the same way a wise man invests soundly and conservatively to protect his wealth.

Since our mythology would have us believe that artists are by nature wild and careless, why talk here in such fiscal terms? Why urge conservatism? Because we are all inwardly wealthy and we can squander our inner wealth the way a fool squanders a fortune.

How do we squander our wealth? To begin with, we show our work too soon and too indiscriminately. We undervalue our valuable writing. We do not qualify our readers the way a bank qualifies an investor. We do not stop to question the aspiring reader's qualifications. In our eagerness to be read, we open the city gates. This is like giving passersby access to our checking account.

Showing our writing to hostile or undiscerning readers is like lending money to people with terrible fiscal pasts. We will not be repaid as we wish. Our work will not be valued. They will respond in dangerous extremes, "brilliant" or "awful." (Long experience teaches that extremes of any kind, high or low, are dangerous to the writing process because they create self-consciousness.) Even if our readers wax enthusiastic, they may do so generically and that, too, is dangerous.

If we overextend ourselves to them—placing in their hands and before their eyes a vulnerable piece of work—we jeopardize our ability to complete the work itself. Our energy gets overdrawn. Energy that should be used for writing gets used instead trying to defend our writing, trying to decide if our critics are "right."

Writing is an act of connection, but it connects the writer first to the Self and secondly to the world. In order to practice self-expression we must keep that in the proper order. We must protect the Self we mean to express. We must treat our writing carefully, as if it were valuable. It *is* valuable.

Writing is communication, yes, but that communication begins internally. The Self communicates to the writer and the writer communicates to the Self. The gist of that communication is what the writer communicates to the world. When the world is allowed to interrupt too early, the Self withdraws. The mind may remain, writing more and more cleverly and defensively, but the soul of the writing will vanish. The spirit of the writing will wobble. What is being said may sound good but it will not sound right. In order for writing to sound right, it must have an inner resonance. In order for writing to have inner resonance, it cannot have too many outer influences. And the influences it does have must be benevolent.

What do I mean by a benevolent influence? I mean an influence that encourages growth rather than uproots it. This was, we forget, what criticism was originally intended to do. When criticism was an art rather than an adversarial position, critics sought to shape and encourage by their comments. Deeply schooled in literary tradition, familiar with the tall trees of literary talents, they could often recognize promising new work the way a skilled forester might spot valuable seedling growth on the forest floor. Today's critics are not trained to give or receive this kind of influence. In our schools and in our media, we are encouraged to "criticize" but we are not shown how to criticize well.

As a writing teacher, it is my experience that if I praise a student's strengths, the weaknesses eventually fall away. If I focus on the weaknesses, the strengths, too, may wobble and even vanish. A young writer is like a young horse. The basic gaits must be developed before too much perfection is required. Just as we would not give over a valuable young horse to just anybody to train, we must not give over our work to just anybody to critique. And by this I do not mean that we must go only to professionals. Too often professionals have their own ax to grind.

An amateur reader can give very valid feedback. (Remember the word "amateur" comes from the verb "amare," to love.) What you want to find in a reader is someone who loves to read and is friendly to the idea of your developing as a writer.

I have done book criticism since I was in my early twenties. It is notoriously hard to write a good review. It is hard to be specific about a book's strengths. It is notoriously easy to write a slam. It is shamefully easy to be specific about a book's weaknesses. For this reason, the "friend" who is reading you may need a little help with how to be a "Friendly Reader."

It is absolutely fair, in giving over a piece of work to be read, to make the proviso: "I want you to tell me what you liked, tell me what you'd like to see more of. Please be specific."

This at least sets the reader off on the right track.

We must write from love and we must choose those to read us who read from love: the love of words. The love of naming our experience must finally be the guiding force in what we put on the page. When we write from fear of criticism, we hamper our stride and we cripple our voice. When we choose as readers those who love to criticize rather than those who love to read, we invite catastrophe.

I have a favorite editor. He inspires me to write freely by reading with the lightest touch possible. He says things to me like, "What about _____? I'd be curious to hear your thinking on that," or "I love this, could you tell me more?" or, gently, "I'm not quite clear on what you mean here, but I'd love to know more." Once in a while he will say, "Fine."

In working with this editor, I have felt so supported in my strongest work that I have found it easy to relinquish parts that are weaker. I have felt myself building on my strengths rather than defending my inevitable weaknesses. Perhaps most valuable of all, I have never felt this editor to be competitive with me. He simply loves good writing and in his enthusiasm for words themselves he inspires me to use them well—perhaps better than I might if I were cringing, waiting to be heavily edited by someone else.

It is difficult to overemphasize the amount of care that must be taken to protect our writing. While we cannot control or in any way guarantee our writing's reception in the public sphere, we can control and to a degree guarantee the reception of our writing in the private sphere. Do not be self-destructive in your choice of early readers.

Terrence, a novelist, wrote brilliantly for years, keeping his early readers to his wife and a few very close friends. Then he acquired a literary agent and began allowing this man to read his early drafts—a catastrophic mistake.

Driven by the market and what he perceived to be "currently" selling, the agent was unable to read the work for its own shape and value. He was quick to ask for drastic revisions not in the direction the work was naturally evolving but in the direction he felt he could sell. Terrence's productivity plummeted. The steady and accomplished production he had enjoyed for years slowed to a crawl and then stopped entirely. He could not write without thinking of what his agent would think and how his agent would want the work altered. Eventually, Terrence could not write at all.

Although we seldom think of it this way, a writer's block is often a very healthy self-protective response on the part of our inner creator to a dangerous threat. Terrence's inner writer refused to have his work misread and mutilated. Only when Terrence finally fired the offending agent did his writer sigh, "Thank God!" and go back to work.

It is very important that we keep a few nurturing readers as friends to our work quite apart from whatever is going on in our publishing life. We need people who are happy to hear a poem or an essay for its own sake and not as career maneuvers. The part of us that writes must be allowed to write freely and not always with an eye to the market. An eye to the market is part of the writing life, but if it is too large a part, it shuts down invention and leads to the blockage of many valuable avenues of exploration which are not—at first blush—commercial.

Eve was an accomplished short-story writer on a publishing roll with a series of stories accepted. She made the mistake of showing a new short story to a competitive fellow writer. "If you publish this story, it will ruin your career," Eve was told ominously.

Eve did not publish the story. She buried the story in a drawer and turned to her also successful journalism as her main writing outlet. Nearly fifteen years would pass before Eve retrieved the story, reread it, told her friends about her discouraging "advice," and then set to work on short stories again.

"But shouldn't a writer be more resilient?" people ask—as well they might.

Whether we "should" be resilient matters less than whether we are more resilient—and many very talented writers are not. The very vulnerability required to be open and creative is a vulnerability that puts our creativity at risk. For this reason, meticulous care must be taken to find "safe" readers and people who can be our "before, during, and after" friends to our work.

With luck and perseverance, we will, one day, have a writing success—perhaps a very large one. When we do, safe friends are even more important. The censor wakes up at any hint of success and starts saying, "What a fluke! You'll never do it again." This is where friends come in, crooning helpfully, "Look. You were a good writer before you got successful and you're a good writer still. Just keep writing."

The actual physical listing of "safe" friends is a very good exercise to undertake. So is the physical listing of dangerous friends. Dangerous friends are expensive readers. They cost Eve fifteen years. They can cost you fifteen years as well. My friend the young Scottish writer is still mysteriously "dry" on story ideas these days. Like Eve, he has channeled his creativity into journalism, where the power of the printed page keeps his friends' opinions at bay.

Gentleness, encouragement, safety—these are the watchwords to be put in place for criticism. I have been writing for thirty years. I have seen more good writing destroyed by bad criticism than I have ever seen bad writing helped by good criticism. I have watched valid and valuable books be picked to pieces by too many editors. I have watched plays start to find their feet, only to be tripped up by too many people contributing fixes.

It is a metaphysical law that "the first rule of magic is containment." Nowhere should that law be more rigorously applied than to our writing.

CONTAINMENT
Initiation Tool

This is another of the "tough love" tools that asks you to make judgments you might normally back off from. Think of this as a surveying tool, one in which you will get the lay of your emotional landscape. This is a tool that you might want to think of as playing scout or lookout for hostile or dangerous elements in your life. Do you see any snipers lurking in the underbrush? Actress Julianna McCarthy calls this tool "Who would you take to the war?"

This tool is best undertaken "out." Take yourself to a safe, interesting, and neutral spot, a café, coffeehouse, or library. You are asked now to engage in sorting, to physically list those people who are friendly to you and your writing and those people who are dangerous to you and your writing. Remember that there are people with good intentions who are detrimental to your work while there are other people whose impact is invigorating. Emotional closeness does not always translate as safety.

Start by numbering one to five. List five people whom you consider safe and supportive. These are people to whom you can show your writing, talk to about your writing, be enthusiastic with about your writing. Do not be discouraged if you come up with fewer than five names. Even one or two people who are genuinely in your corner is an enormous step in the right direction.

1.

2.

3.

4.

5.

Next number from one to five again. This time physically list five people with whom it is dangerous to share your writing. This is a trickier list. On it go the people who give you mixed messages, those who talk to you about "the odds" of your success, those who are either competitive or frightened by your success. On this list be certain to place people who blow hot and cold, sometimes encouraging you and other times discouraging you.

1.

2.

3.

4.

5.

Reading over both lists, get an overview of your writing environment. Does your life, as it is currently constituted, encourage or discourage your writing? Is there one person on your positive list whom you could safely designate as a Friendly Reader, someone capable of reading and enjoying your writing out of a love of letters? Select your best candidate.

After you return home from your writing expedition, call your potential Friendly Reader. Explain that you are becoming more and more serious in your writing practice and that you would like to ask them to function not as a critic but as a reader, someone with whom you can share your work. If they accept, thank them and explain that they will be a part, a valued part, of your writer's life cycle. You may want to schedule a formal coffee date to celebrate.

SOUND

WRITING IS SENSUAL. We often talk about the importance of visual acuity, but we seldom talk about the auditory component of writing. We talk about a writing voice but seldom about the importance of literal sounds in the sound it makes.

As I write, it is a hot but breezy afternoon and I am perched on my back porch. My apple trees are shaken by wind. Their leaves make a distinct whir as they fan the air. A smaller, dryer tree, closer in to the porch, has a dry paper whisper to its leaves as they nod and swish, brushing the adobe wall. My chow dog, Golden King, is rooting in the garden dirt with grunts of determination as he digs, digs, digs. The new rottweiler puppy is panting from the heat. A half mile below my land, down on the highway, a truck is changing gears. Closer in, a pickup barrels and rattles on my rutted dirt road. An insistent cricket chirps from my pasture. Now there is a chorus of crickets. A raucous, in-your-face magpie baits the sultry dogs from the pasture fence. I have Tibetan bells and pipe chimes hung from the rafters on this porch. The wind sets them ringing a high feminine counterpart to the guttural pickups gunning past.

We talk about music in writing but we seldom focus on the music all around us. The world is alive with song—the city's cacophonous jazzed-up symphony and the variable pastoral of my country life.

It is an idyllic summer afternoon. A teenage boy roars past on a dirt bike. It's loud enough that even the magpies flee to cover, complaining (loudly) about the racket from the branches of the small dead tree halfway across my pasture.

The new puppy is five months old. Her bark is already larger than my house. The bumblebee whirring above my head sounds annoyed by all her clamor. The horses walking closer in have set her off: "What are you?" she barks. Domenica's white Arab, Walter, tosses his mane at her sound.

Sometimes, to start a piece of writing, or to ground a piece of writing into definite reality, it takes sound as well as sight. The aluminum dog dish just went skittering across the stone porch floor. The puppy's bark has a worried woof in it as those large beings, horses, drift closer still. A red pickup thrums down the road, and what's this? An out-of-town visitor cruises the field's lower road in a fancy sports car. All the dogs take note—the rottweiler's basso profundo to Maxwell, my Lhasa apso's tinny tenor.

Our lives have sound tracks. We seldom look at that as a literal term: Sound leaves tracks in our consciousness. When we trace our hand across a page, the scratch of the pen can record the tracks of other sounds as well. When we do, our writing becomes more sound.

I was once asked to write a movie about Elvis Presley. He was the King, an American phenomenon that changed the sound of our world. I remembered early Elvis—his urgency and heat—but in the writing of my movie I chose for myself a personal sound track of early Bruce Springsteen albums that I kept playing and replaying as my scenes unfurled. I wanted my Elvis movie to have youth, heat, and energy, a poignant Americana that I found most vividly for myself in the sounds of Springsteen and his E Street Band. Was this "translation" heresy? Oh, probably. But it worked.

For many writers, baroque music, particularly Bach, is what works. For writers involved in long and complex pieces of logical writing, Mozart is said to actually raise and steady the I.Q.—as well as one's math skills. The propulsive drumbeat of rock and roll drives some writers like a powerful engine. For other writers, the more evanescent and hypnotic effect of flute music sets them to musing.

One writer's potion is another writer's poison. Some writers cannot write without soft jazz unspooling in the background. Other writers cannot write to jazz because they become distracted, listening. There are many writers who use no music at all.

Ambient music—green forest meadows of birdsong and wind or the low and soothing roll of waves—makes a perfect writing background for some writers. Others have been known to set a slowly ticking metronome—which would drive still another writer to distraction.

Some of the happiest and freest writing I have ever done was produced while listening to music by Tim Wheater. One story is particularly worth telling.

Wheater and I were high in the Rocky Mountains recording an album of prayers. I found that for me the intense electrical fields of the studio were very disconcerting. I had to leave. We had parked the car just outside the studio door. I repaired to the car to escape the electricity. Right before I retreated, Wheater said to me, "You really should write two little books. One of prayers to animals and one of prayers for children."

"You write them!" I retorted. "I'm busy enough."

Wheater went back in the studio to lay down more flute tracks. I perched in the car to continue writing this book, but it was not to be. Something in the flute music set my mind humming. I had an idea for a short prayer, To the God of Ant. I wrote it down and was given another short prayer, To the God of Flea. Within fifteen minutes it was obvious that prayers were queued up like airplanes waiting to land. I settled in in the car's front seat with the studio's little Tibetan dog, Rhythm, settled beside me. While Wheater played solo after haunting solo, I wrote prayer after prayer. Within two days I had fifty-two prayers and Wheater had finished our album.

The hot afternoon is winding down. The birdsong has changed shifts. Song sparrows and finches are coming in for an early evening meal. The puppy has found a bone—bones, bones of all kinds, turn up everywhere here in New Mexico. This bone, a lamb's bone, makes a small racketing sound as it's ground in the puppy's teeth. I'm about to grab it, fearing it will splinter, when the puppy loses interest—a banging screen door caught his ear. The pup is distracted by the sound and so moves on.

The conscious use of sound in our writing—like a great sound track in a film—cues the unconscious. It brings to bear a host of associations that are more subtly and acutely felt than visual images alone. Sound makes our writing "sound" in the many senses of the word.

SOUND
Initiation Tool

This is a tool I would like you to do in two parts. In Step One, you are asked to observe the world of sound you are actually living in. In Step Two, you are asked to use sound to expand that world.

Set aside one full hour of writing time. This tool should be done "in." You are asked to preplan and then execute a "sonic" writing date.

First of all, settle in comfortably where you are. Get very still. What do you hear? I am surrounded by birdsong, the distant rumble of a truck, a sudden sharp car horn. There is the faint soughing of the wind. My refrigerator gives off a whir . . . What sounds are in your immediate environment? Which do you allow yourself to hear? Which do you tune out? Note them all.

Now choose for yourself a piece of what I call "expansion" music. This is music that urges you to feel large and adventurous. For many people, "Chariots of Fire" is such a piece of music. For me, I have often used Tim Wheater's album *Green Dream* with its spirit of Celtic quest.

Cue up your expansion music, settle in to write, and let yourself dream on the page. You are asked to envision an expanded life. What would your "ideal" look like in the following areas?

- Spirituality
- Friendships
- Work life

- Living space
- Vacation/Adventure
- Creative projects

Take a full hour and allow yourself to spend ten minutes or so envisioning each "improved" area.

I Would Love to
Write, But . . .

THIS AFTERNOON I HAD a phone conversation with a woman who used to be an editor at a children's press. She was talking to me because she wanted to write but wasn't writing.

"So why aren't you writing?" I asked her.

In the past I had read articles by this woman—lively, well-written articles, and I had received letters—lively and well-written letters. Talent clearly was not the issue. Confidence was.

"I'm afraid I am just not original enough," the woman told me. "I'm afraid that my ideas are trite and I just don't know it. I am afraid of doing a lot of work only to have people say 'It's been done before.' "

"Stop right there," I told the woman. "Everything has been done before. Don't worry about being new. There is no 'new.' Worry about being human."

I asked the woman to think over whether she herself demanded that the work she read be wholly new.

"Well, actually, no, when you put it that way," she answered.

"I don't think 'new' is what we connect to in writing," I told her. "I think human is."

"So what's human?"

"I think it's whatever you are truly, humanly interested in."

"Well, I am interested in animals and I have collected hundreds of animal stories which I'd really like to write about, but then I think, 'Maybe no one's interested in animals except me.'"

"Do you really think that's true?"

"Actually, when you put it that way—no. *All Creatures Great and Small* was all about animals and lots of people loved it."

"So you actually know that your subject is good and you're still not writing. Why really?"

"Well, I guess I am scared of doing all that work for nothing. I mean, what if I write all my stories and no one buys them?"

"You would still have had the delight of having written them."

"That's true."

The woman did not sound convinced. Perhaps we can blame it on her years in publishing, but she seemed unable to connect to the idea of writing as process instead of product. So steeped was she in professionalism that she had lost the notion of writing for amateurs— that is, writing from love.

"I think I want some kind of guarantee," the woman went on. "I am afraid of looking foolish."

About a month ago I had dinner with a lawyer. We started talking about our work and I told him that I wrote many things just for the joy of writing them.

"Wait a minute," the lawyer said, genuinely aghast. "You mean you write these things on spec?"

I have never thought of writing for love as writing on spec. I have always felt that the payoff in self-respect more than equaled the cost in time and energy. I have also found that much of what I wrote for love later sold for very solid money.

"Do you like writing?" I asked the woman.

"Actually, when I let myself do it, I love it."

"Then why ask to be paid to do something you love? Separate the two issues. Write for love and worry about being paid later."

"I could, couldn't I?"

She certainly could. Most of us certainly could if we would just give ourselves permission. Unfortunately, most of us do not give ourselves permission. We are waiting for someone else to come along and stamp our passport. We want official validation that we are "really" writers. The truth is, we need to give that permission, that validation, ourselves.

When we think about publishing, we think in terms of lucky breaks. We do not think in terms of making our own luck, manufacturing our own breaks. And yet, a startling percentage of the books that make it to our best-seller lists began as someone's stubborn idea, stubbornly self-published. *The Celestine Prophecy* is only one such book, a recent example. And, quite apart from best-seller lists and "beating the odds," there is the solid satisfaction of the modest yet fully realized success of seeing the book in our mind become the book held in our hand.

For many of us, bestsellerdom is not even what we are after. We are after the joy of being read. With the advent of computer publishing, self-publishing can be done on a relative shoestring. The existence of the World Wide Web has also created a market of on-line storytelling that is another viable outlet for many people.

Many of us scare ourselves out of beginning our writing projects by imagining with terror the bad reviews they will eventually receive. I have found that enlisting one Friendly Reader can allow me to jump-start a project on which I have been stalled. I wrote a detective novel that I read to my friend Ellen Longo in installments, over lunch. Ellen's "What happens next?" kept me writing.

For many writers, this is where a writing friend can be an indispensable ally. Both of you can agree to meet and write simultaneously on the projects that frighten you. I have often used this technique with my friend Mark Bryan, and we both have the resulting books to show for it.

This is the precise point where writing is best broken down into a one-day-at-a-time, one-page-at-a-time process. We do not need the courage to write a whole novel. We need the courage only to write on the novel today. We do not need the courage to finish and publish a novel all in one fell swoop. All we need is the courage to do the next right thing. Today's pages may yield tomorrow's editing job and next month's design job, but just for today all we need to do is write.

"I do know some stories I think a lot of people would enjoy," the lady editor finally volunteers, sounding somewhat brighter. "Maybe I should start them."

"Don't start them. Start one of them."

"That's all?"

"That's all it ever takes."

I W O U L D L O V E T O
W R I T E , B U T . . .
Initiation Tool

Set aside a full hour's writing time. Get comfortable and then number from one to five. List five trite, clichéd, and heartwarming topics that are very "human." The goal of your list is to come up with what you might call the *"Reader's Digest"* quotient, that is, a topic almost anyone can relate to. For example:

- My most beloved pet
- My favorite relative
- My best holiday
- My most gratifying moment
- My most inspiring teacher

Choose one of your topics. Set pen to page and allow yourself to be detailed and human for one hour. Do not worry about being hip. Do not worry about being sentimental. Recall to mind in precise detail what was memorable and lovable about your subject. This is a "cup" you are to share with a Friendly Reader.

DRIVING

I OWN A '65 PICKUP truck named Louise. When I drive
her she bucks over the rutted dirt roads like a stiff-legged bronco.
Louise has a windshield big enough to hold New Mexico. She can
take in a mesa of sagebrush horizon to horizon. In a snowstorm she is
practically a cabin on wheels. You do get the picture through her
window.

I have a drive to write and I do drive to write. I am very aware
that the art of writing devours images and that if I am going to write
deeply, frequently, and well, I must keep my inner pond of images
very well stocked. When I want to restock my images, I get behind
the wheel of my car.

In addition to Louise, I own Bon Bon, a bright red four-wheel-
drive Oldsmobile Bravado built on a Blazer chassis. Bon Bon can go
anywhere, and that's where I take her. For the past week we have
been having spectacularly showy sunsets. Three weeks ago the
canopy was orchid, fuchsia, and deep purple. Last night it was a wall
of solid gold. Spotting that wall, I grabbed my daughter Domenica,
my friend James Nave, the poet, and said, "C'mon, let's get a drive."

The town of Taos is modern enough to sport Video Casa and
several spots for good chocolate mousse, but it is a town built in an
old agrarian valley and you can quickly leave the town behind.
Loaded into Bon Bon, Domenica, Nave, and I headed due west

toward the sunset on a small blacktop road. Immediately we came hard up on a tractor hauling home a bailer after a day in the fields. Past the tractor, we were suddenly eyeball to eyeball with a hell-for-leather pickup using our side of the road. A quick swerve of the wheel, a near enough miss, and then traffic was behind us and the sunset ahead. Bands of copper, bronze, and pewter now showcased the gold sun. This is the molten light filmmakers call "golden hour."

Taos Valley is bigger on sheep than on cattle. In the dusky light the fluffy sheep looked like luminous grounded clouds. In a dark green neatly squared pasture, a snow-white Arabian stallion looked carved like an ivory talisman. His companion, a chiseled buckskin, glowed brightly, a burnished gold.

Nosing north on the Calle Medio, Bon Bon glowed fiery red as a cherry lozenge. The Sacred Mountain dead ahead bulked dark and ominous; its folded flanks gilded but darker than gold. Fifteen minutes driving north, sunset on the left, then fifteen minutes driving south, sunset on the right, and then I maneuvered Bon Bon home. As a writer, I eat with my eyes, and that sumptuous sunset sated my appetite. Today I am hungry to write.

Four years ago, before we knew he was dying, my father and I set off cross-country from Sarasota, Florida, along the gulf, across Texas on a long diagonal, and home into New Mexico. I started the trip after a long year's teaching. Working with my class on the subject of "creative U-turns," I'd remembered and told the story of how I'd begun as a short-story writer, like my friend Eve and, like Eve, abandoned that art form when my best friend discouraged me. I knew from past experience that telling creative wounds helped to heal them. I knew from past experience that driving filled me with writing fuel, but I was still unprepared for what happened.

My father and I were midway across Texas in his snow-white Probe with his black Scottie dog named Blue. We were enjoying the truck stops with their Patsy Cline jukeboxes and biscuits with redeye gravy. We were just pulling out of one, when a voice in my head said clearly, "Karen's new life began ten miles west of the Pecos River, that's where she said to Jerry, 'Pull over. Now.'"

I grabbed for a notebook and began chasing the voice. My father nosed the little car deep into the Texas panhandle while I scribbled at his side. Jackrabbits, rattlers, vultures, coyotes— my characters were more interesting than all of them. We were doing a cool eighty but my hand was flying at the speed of light. I was quite literally driven to write. Before we pulled into a motel for the night, I had a finished short story. Twenty more would speed through my hand faster than my father's car gobbled the white center line.

Driving kicks over my writing engine. Driving lets me write full throttle. Driving drives me to the page.

"Why is it," director Steven Spielberg once mused, "that I get my best ideas when I'm driving?"

Artists, artists of all stripes, devour images in order to produce. Driving, with its constant inflow of images, catalyzes active creative thought.

When I lived in Manhattan, I had a beat-up dull gold Blazer that I kept in a parking lot on Ninth Avenue. It was dumb—and expensive—having a car in Manhattan, but for me it was very, very smart. I would load Domenica, then a toddler, and her dog, Calla Lily, a snow-white royal standard poodle, into the car. I would nose onto the West Side Highway and push north along the Hudson with my eyes devouring the gifts of space and light. As a writer and a person, I need to see distance. (I also kept an Appaloosa horse in Manhattan which Domenica and I would ride double to the top of the highest hill in Central Park.) Heading north along the glistening snake of river, I would rough out screenplays, "watch" plays as they unfurled to my mind's eye. Heading into the green tunnels of the Merritt Parkway, my citified, city-fried mind would get a heady dose of creative oxygen and head back home nurtured by new ideas.

Writing, for me, is a Zen pursuit. I focus on the page by focusing on life. I focus on life by focusing on the ribbon of road unspooling gift by gift before my eyes.

The Long, Quiet Highway, Buddhist Natalie Goldberg entitled her memoir of a writing life. John Nichols, who gave us *The Sterile Cuckoo, Wizard of Loneliness,* and *The Milagro Beanfield War,* among others, claims to have written some of his best stuff careening along New Mexico highways in his pickup, one eye on the highway, one hand on the wheel, and one sentence at a time on the scrap of paper trapped on his blue-jeaned thigh. Poet James Nave, an incorrigible driver known to log up to 100,000 miles a year criss-crossing the country to teach poetry, live, went so far as to name his dog Traveler. His signature poem, the one on posters, is titled "The Road."

More than miles pass beneath our vision when we go out driving. Focused on the road, our pressing psychological dilemmas become roadside attractions, slipping their weight from our consciousness as we notice a ruby-red model T, a cockeyed diner that looks worth trying.

When I was writing *The Vein of Gold,* I was walking through the slow death of my father. Grounded by lung cancer and emphysema, he was no longer able to make the long road trips that were our favorite. I went to visit him, took him on some fifty-mile jaunts. After the visit, I splurged on a long, scenic train ride west to home. The miles on that train, the images unfolding outside the window, became the thoughts, realizations, and tools of *The Vein of Gold.*

Not everybody drives a car— but maybe all writers should. Barring that, we need nod, at least, to the notion that seeing distance helps us to go the distance as well.

DRIVING
Initiation Tool

The goal of this tool is to fill your writing well with images. You will often find that the conscious intake of images gives you a sense of well-being and abundance. You may also find that tricky plot points suddenly untangle as new solutions suggest themselves. Enjoy!

For those of you who have a car, this is a driving assignment. Take one to two hours and set off to explore some smaller roads. Get off the freeways and thruways and let yourself look at farmlands or community neighborhoods. Notice the architectural style and vintage. Imagine life in the places you pass by. Get off the beaten track.

For those of you who do not have a car, take a bus ride, a boat cruise around Manhattan, a train ride. If necessary, ride a bike. The object is to let a flow of images wash over you, to eat with your eyes. Take in passing churches, cemeteries, diners, and golf courses. Think about the dailiness and the variety of human experience. Let yourself be like an empty beaker set out during a rainstorm. Gently fill.

Roots

It is the Fourth of July, high summer. On the table where I write, I've got one worn-thin horseshoe, a nosegay of rambling roses, red, an adobe bird planter, and a mano ponderosa power candle. Nearby, four of the five household dogs loll in the tall grasses. Except for the need to be vigilant about snakes, everything is peaceful here. Two years ago, after my father died, I built this miniature meadow. With the help of a local artisan, I made a small adobe fishpond, a memento of my father's love of water. Every day, after our afternoon walk in the sagebrush, my dogs come home and plunge into the pond. Right now the pond's surface is serenely rippled by a high fragrant wind that has set heavy bells and light chimes ringing all through the fields of this old Spanish neighborhood. Surrounded by all of this tranquillity, I have a restless heart. Even as a child I remember the Fourth of July as a troublesome holiday. As a writer, I find holidays often disturbing, not liberating, in their disruption of tempo, their open-ended time.

Very often, when people think about writing, they picture the writer's life being best when it contains vast savannahs of freedom, huge bolts of structureless, unused time.

I'm not so certain about that. In fact, writing benefits from other commitments. Writing responds well to some gentle scheduling. A day job not only promotes solvency, it promotes creativity as well.

T. S. Eliot worked in a bank. Raymond Chandler sold insurance. A great many writers, myself among them, have taught school. Richard Cole, author of *Stairway to Heaven,* a book about Led Zeppelin, road-manages rock and roll groups as his day job.

All of these jobs create a flow not only of money but also of experience into the writer's life. Writers need to live in the world.

Poet James Nave has owned a pizza restaurant, a mountain biking store, and was co-founder of Poetry Alive! which sent poets out to teach poetry, live, to six million schoolchildren. Throughout all these peripatetic occupations, Nave has written. His poems are sourced in the rich flow of the multicolored life he leads.

One of our great fears, as writers, is that we will be boring. Give us too much time and we do run the risk of boredom. Give us too much self-involvement and we lose our involvement with the world. Yes, then we are boring.

Writer/intuitive Sonia Choquette leads a demanding life. She gives spiritual readings six hours a day, raises two daughters with her husband, Patrick, teaches workshops on intuition and manifestation and—oh, yes—writes a steady stream of books on the side. Sonia's books, like her life, are filled with people. She is heart deep in the river of humanity, and a humanizing grounded compassion flows through her prose. Sonia's busy life is her root system.

In order to bloom, all of us need a root system. Just as a regular practice of writing roots us firmly in our lives, a regular life roots us firmly in our writing. Those long sabbaticals everyone lusts after so they can be truly productive seldom yield the promised result. Too often the yawning vistas of time yield self-involved work that yawns on the page. Writers writing about what to write are writers for whom something isn't right. When we center our writing lives on our writing instead of on our lives, we leach both our lives and our writing of the nutrients they require.

Henry is—or was—a productive and prolific novelist, a man of far-flung interests and friends. About three years ago, he began slowly and steadily shrinking the size of his life, telling himself that he needed to focus more on his writing—that it needed more care and time and attention than it had required for the past three decades.

Rather than blooming under Henry's focused attention, his writing life withered like a plant left unwatered in the glare of the sun.

"I can't come out," Henry said to dinner invitations. "I have to work."

"I don't go to movies anymore," Henry said to movie invitations.

For the first time in thirty years, Henry stopped being hired to write movies. His editor responded to two of his short novels with the ominous note, "You've been over this territory before"—and Henry had.

With the best of intentions, despite years of experience that might have taught him that his writing life flourished when he focused not on writing but on life, Henry had unwittingly cut himself off from his own root system. He became not a steady stream of freely flowing ideas, but a stagnant pond of recycled ideas and insights.

"I don't know why it's so hard," Henry told me recently. "I can't live like this and I can't write like this."

"So come to the movies," I cajoled. "Come to dinner."

Little by little, Henry reluctantly allowed himself to be coaxed back out. The last I heard, he was writing more freely and had an editor interested in a novella.

"I can't come to dinner. I've got houseguests," Henry reported the last time I talked to him. His life was one more time overflowing—and so was his writing.

Dark, heavy storm clouds are clustering on the flanks of the sacred mountain. The fireworks of nature will one more time outshine the firecrackers of man. It's time to walk the dogs through the sagebrush or forget about walking the dogs. Lightning in New Mexico falls in great golden bolts. There's a science fiction quality to the storms out here, as though UFOs really are dropping landing beams. Thunder is crackling in the distance. The smell of water is on the wind. That and the high, sharp smell of kerosene from somebody's backyard barbecue mixing with the sage. It is the Fourth of July, and before all this freedom gets to me, I will walk my dogs through the sagebrush, just beating the storm. Then, once again, I will write.

ROOTS
Initiation   Tool

This is a tool of conscious self-cherishing. You are once again asked to look at yourself as a character and this time to observe yourself making a hero's choices.

Set aside one hour of writing time, "in" or "out." Look back along your life—what I call your Narrative Time Line—and choose an episode in which you exercised your freedom of choice to a positive outcome. Maybe you married the "wrong" boy who was right for you. Maybe you moved to a new city or a new job. Maybe you left a marriage, adopted a child—or even a new dog. Whatever risk you chose, choose it again, and celebrate it and yourself on the page. This assignment is a celebration both of freedom and of courage.

ESP

THE SKY THIS AFTERNOON is dark and forbidding—the perfect sky for writing an essay on the role of psychic phenomena in writing. Let me begin by saying I consider psychic phenomena to be a normal part of life. I do not ascribe to the Johnny-come-lately school of rationalism, which would have us believe only in the solid world of five senses and the things they can easily explain. It is my belief that writing is a spiritual practice and that the world of spirit is far larger, and more variable, than the physical world—and every bit as real. Perhaps more real, I might argue.

Every time I put my hand to the page, I am altering the energy that flows through my life. "In the beginning was the word," spiritual tradition tells us, and I believe that to be true. "Through every word runs power," advises spiritual teacher Sonia Choquette. "That power is real whether you believe in it or not."

I have been an active writer for three decades—long enough to know better. I've been asked to write about killers and had friends of their victims show up at my door. I've written movies where I "made up" characters, only to have real-life versions of them turn up sometime later, identical in every detail. I believe that when a writer focuses attention on a topic, we are posing a question to the universe that asks: "What can you tell me about this?" Quite often the answer is "A good deal—and from many different sources."

In metaphysical circles, it is believed that all the information of the past, present, and future is stored someplace called "the Akashic Records." A sort of celestial library, the Akashic Records are what psychic "readers" read. It is my belief that as writers we, too, often access information beyond our normal realm of knowing. We ask, "How would this character behave?" and the answer that we hear is often grounded in a level of detail and veracity that withstands the test of time.

About fifteen years ago, before the term and the concept "serial killer" entered our collective consciousness, I wrote a movie about just such a man. A few weeks into undertaking it, my path intersected a political activist who was working with the FBI to computerize data on a national level to help catch multiple murderers. I told him I was writing about such a killer and described the character as I had come to know him. My expert new friend listened quietly. Finally he drew a deep breath.

"You are very, very accurate," he said.

I wrote the movie, titled *Normal Murder,* and about a year later came across a book detailing the idiosyncrasies of serial killers. The book listed fifteen traits ranging from religion to automobile make. Of the fifteen traits, thirteen of them belonged to the character I had invented. This was more than a high enough ratio to give me pause. "Maybe," I thought, "I've missed my calling and I'd actually have made quite a good sleuth."

Maybe. But what I am is a writer. It is my belief that many writers routinely ask questions that the universe willingly answers.

A friend of mine is a young playwright. For the past year, she has been writing a play about date rape. It is a tough, canny play—and the universe has sent the writer an uncanny number of clues that her writing is on the right track.

"I had my rapist attack two girls who were close friends but did not tell each other what had happened. When I was writing my second draft of the play, I held auditions for a workshop production. I encountered two girls, friends, who told me I had written their story."

There are many forms of reincarnation. All of us lead multiple lives. My characters are perhaps secret selves, parts of me and my friends that need rebirthing. Or, as it sometimes seems, maybe it works the other way, the way it can when I am writing. Then it seems that the characters are telling the story, that they know the plot, that they are the ones who reveal the twists and turns of what will happen to me and to them. They are, it feels most times, writing through me. I am their device, a clever one, that serves them.

A month ago, my beloved friend David disappeared down the rabbit hole of his work, and I had a disturbing dream. I was in a Nazi household. I was a spy. They'd discovered me. They were coming to get me. I had two poison pills in my hand. I was about to take them, to choose death and avoid torture, when I saw a door mysteriously ajar. I snatched the moment, bolted for the door, and ran for a car parked a hundred yards down the street. If I could just make it to that car, if I could just slip into the rumble seat . . .

I woke up, but I had seen myself: a tall, willowy girl with reddish-gold bobbed hair.

I lurched bolt upright. This was no ordinary dream. Instantly I thought of my missing friend, David. Had I known him then, in that lifetime? I knew I had. He had contrived to leave the street door ajar. We were in the Resistance together.

"I will not go back there," I heard myself say. "I will not write about that."

But David stayed away, working, and the girl in the dream would not go away, and I began to know the story that wanted to come through.

Yes, David my friend was missing, but in the story my friend was supposed to be missing. He had important work to do in the underground. So had I. And so, because my friend was gone and I had to do something to make me happy, I opened the door to the story the dream had told me.

"It's about time," my character all but said. She began speaking clearly and volubly. Every day, pen in hand, I met her and let her talk to me about her missing lover, her scary work, the terror she felt and fought. Our lives braided together.

A prowler at my New Mexico windows became the paranoia at hers. The young rottweiler puppy in my household became her beloved dog, Lola. Her lover who promised he would come back for her, whom she had to trust despite fear, became my missing friend, David. His necessary disappearance underground into his work became literally the Underground as he provided the character for my character.

"You love him because he is dangerous," I remembered his telling me of Bob, my feckless and reckless young horse.

I came to understand that was an accurate assessment of my character's love for her resistance lover and perhaps an accurate assessment of me and my love for my elusive friend as well. The little book grew.

My days took on a pattern. Morning Pages. Off to the gym. Back to work with Mark Bryan on a book we were writing together. Slipping off for a late afternoon rendezvous with my own secret book. Dinner with my daughter. Another quick round of writing before bed. Nights made restless by the uncaught prowler in the neighborhood, nights given to me in which I understood more of my character's fear, the actions she took by necessity.

I had to get an alarm system. Mount motion detector lights. I had to all but raze the foliage embracing my house—hiding places for danger. I wept over the changes being wrought. I understood the slow and terrible fist of fear. I yearned for the time a few months back when the days were sunny and my friend David and I tossed faxes back and forth like paper airplanes. Now he was "lost" in Europe, fifteen countries in four weeks. I was left with stormy weather on every front.

"It was a dark, stormy night"—and so I wrote about it.

Someday, when the little book is done, I will show my friend the silk purse I made from his departure. I hope he will not mind the liberties I took, making him a lover and not just a friend, making us the prototypes for two other people who perhaps orchestrated our meeting so that I would see them and allow them once more to be born.

As I write this, the sky is entirely overcast. Thunder rumbles through Taos Valley. Some showy lightning bolts are flashing off the east flank of the Sacred Mountain. The wind, through the trees and grasses, makes a papery-dry hissing sound. I find myself just a little edgy.

"Not all psychic phenomena are spooky," my friend Sonia Choquette reminds me. "Quite the contrary. Most guidance is quite benevolent and helpful."

Of course, this kind of guidance is the type most writers discuss as coincidence. But is it?

When I was writing my musical, *Avalon,* I was interested in the idea of higher forces involving sound, music, and plant life. One night, as I was going to bed, I grabbed two titles from my metaphysical bookshelves, where I had perhaps two hundred books. Settling in to read, I was startled to find that both of my reading "choices" dealt specifically, and at length, with the precise topics of my play. Concepts I thought I had made up appeared right there in black and white as other people's spiritual experiences. "What about these topics?" my writing had asked the Universe.

"You're on the right track," had come the mysterious reply.

"Ask, believe, receive," Stella Merrill Mann shorthands the formula for spiritual manifestation. As writers, we ask questions about a subject, believe what our imagination tells us, and receive very accurate information. Is all of the support, all of the information we receive, really just so much coincidence? I don't think so.

Over the years, I have slowly, even reluctantly, developed a faith in the answers that come when we directly address the Universe on the page. For myself, I do it formally, asking the questions I need answered in direct, black and white ways.

Q. What else do readers need to know about ESP?

A. If they will try asking questions and then listening for answers, they themselves will be startled by the guidance they receive.

"I was very wary," says Allison. "The idea of posing questions on the page struck me as like playing with a Ouija board. I don't know why, but I was afraid I was asking for possession or something. Actually, it turned out that what I got was more like self-possession."

Beginning with questions of plot and plotting in her work—to which she "heard" very direct and useful answers—Allison moved on to asking questions of plot and plotting regarding her life.

"I would pose a question on the page and then listen and write down what I heard. I had to be careful not to censor, to just obediently write down what I heard. When I did, I got a great deal of information that later proved to be objectively true, although at the time I had no way of knowing that it was accurate."

Over the years, I, like Allison, have learned to "go to the page" with questions regarding my work. I have asked for and received guidance on what to do next, on how to do better what it was that I was already doing. Posing the question, "listening," I often "heard" answers that seemed to come from a source different from my normal consciousness. I would receive directives and advice that surprised me. Feeling resistance, but wanting to have an open mind, I would move out in faith on the suggested directions, only to find that the advice was sound and that my work benefited. As a result of guidance, I wrote many things I otherwise would never have considered.

It was guidance from the page that led me to undertake a musical, *Avalon*. "Surely I would know if I were musical," my skeptic piped up at the suggestion that I would be writing a musical. Nonetheless, I undertook writing music and have now had my musical *Avalon* produced to happy response.

It was guidance from the page that urged me into writing prayer books—not a direction I would ever have seen myself taking. At this writing, I have written four prayer books and count them among my better work.

It was guidance from the page that told me I was to undertake the novella, an outmoded form, that I would find pleasure and success in writing them. I have since written three novellas and found writing each of them to be a very enjoyable process.

For me, the process of taking guidance on work matters has now extended itself into asking for and receiving written guidance on personal matters as well. When I am in a quandary over what I should be doing or what is the underlying meaning or value of events, I will take to the page and ask to be given a "reading" on the events at hand. I have for ten years now written out and saved these readings. Repeatedly, their "take" on things has proven to be correct.

(I nonetheless, even in the face of considerable experience, retain an exhausting, "show-me" attitude—which they do. Most recently, they assured me a dark and disturbing novel of mine would be bought and published—as it has been.)

It is my belief that all of us are naturally intuitive and that writing opens an inner spiritual doorway that gives us access to information both personally and professionally that serves us well. I call this information "guidance," lacking another word and not feeling, since it now seems so normal and matter-of-fact, that "ESP" is the term that best applies.

"But, Julia, do you honestly believe we can all ask questions and be guided in and by our writing?"

"Yes. I do."

"What if the guidance is wishful thinking? How do you know it's real?"

I suggest that all writers should consciously and concretely experiment with guided writing. Questions should be posed, and then the answers received should be weighed against concrete experience. E.g.: The guidance said this would happen—and it did.

It is my considerable experience, based on my own life experience and that of my many students, that an open mind, a spirit of scientific inquiry, and the willingness to delve into the unknown can lead all writers to an unexpected inner resource that will greatly enrich both their lives and their work. This is not my theory. It is my objective experience.

ESP
Initiation Tool

You do not need to wait for a dark and stormy night to use this tool. Set aside an hour's writing time, settle in, and write for one full hour on the following questions:

1.   Do you believe in God? Describe your belief or lack of belief. Is your God friendly to creative endeavors? Describe a God that could be. Once you allow for the possibility of such a benevolent force, you may begin to see evidence of one.

2.   Do you believe in angels or other higher helping forces? Describe your belief or your disbelief. Again, once you open the door to the idea that there may be higher inspirational forces, you may encounter them.

3. Have you had any experiences related to writing that *could* be described as uncanny or possibly connected to ESP?

4. Are you willing to experiment with the use of ESP in the form of synchronicity in your writing?

5. Name one topic on which you would like more information for your writing. For one week be alert to any "coincidental" flow of information that comes your way.

CHEAP TRICKS

How do you do it?" people often ask me, meaning, "How do you stay prolific and productive?"

"I use a lot of cheap tricks," I tell them. I am not kidding.

Tired as we may be of hearing about our "inner children," I do know that the part of me that writes is young, vulnerable, and easily swayed. My writer can be easily discouraged, as today, by someone's passing comment. Conversely, my writer can be easily cheered, encouraged, even bribed. I use a lot of cheap tricks to bribe my writer into production. For example, I have multiple "writing stations" scattered throughout my house and, for that matter, my town.

I am writing at the moment in the small pumpkin-colored room I call "the cockpit." I use this room to call New York and L.A. It is my business headquarters and I use it whenever I want to be crisp, focused, and no-nonsense—the mood of this essay, as it happens.

In addition to the cockpit, I have my usual writing room. It is a light, airy corner room with lilac walls and lace-curtained windows. Just outside one of the windows is the songbirds' feeder. The other windows look south to the foothills writer Natalie Goldberg described as "two elephants kissing." I use the writing room for long stints at the computer. Its romantic feeling softens the task at hand.

At the back of the house, on the covered porch, I write at an old aqua picnic table facing directly toward the Sacred Mountain; that's where I go when writing feels uphill and I need some spiritual inspiration.

To the front of the house, behind adobe walls, lies my fourth writing station, the Meadow. It's the small grassy courtyard filled with wildflowers and a fishpond. The meadow is where I write when I need to feel pampered and as if I have a life beyond my writing.

Multiple writing stations is a cheap trick. It keeps my writer from feeling cornered or like a child being sent to its room. Changing stations with my moods, I bribe myself into writing when I might not feel like it. I move station to station some days, or write three days at a stretch at the picnic table, other times rotating briskly a station per day.

When nowhere in my house feels like a good spot to write, I take my notebook and head to town. Writing in cafés is another cheap trick. For years I wrote books longhand in Dori Vinella's café, where I was often catercorner across the room from novelist John Nichols up to the same thing. Now that Dori has closed her café, I head to the Trading Post Café, where I hole up at a corner table and let the hubbub of the busy boîte bubble around me.

As a young poet, I found my writing niche high in Georgetown Library under the baleful gaze of a stone gargoyle. These days, the sunny rooms at the Taos library are a welcome escape from the too busy phones that sometimes disturb me at home. For me, the trick is to find someplace busy enough to be lively but also respectful enough of writing that you get some done. Coffee bars work. So do the other kind. For that matter, waiting rooms work, and I have a fondness for the chairs in hotel lobbies. As I've said, my writer is a little kid, and you know how much little kids like to be a part of life. Writing stations outside my home help my writer from feeling isolated or punished.

So does another cheap trick, the sandwich call. When I feel like I just can't write, I pick up the phone and call Susan, Sonia, Martha, Dori, Laura, or Alex. "Stick me in the prayer pot," I tell them. "I don't feel like writing, but I'm going to. I'll call you when I'm done." After that call, I fill my time with writing. That done, I phone back and make the second half of the sandwich, "Thanks for the support. I've lived to write another day."

"But isn't that cheating?" I am sometimes asked. "Aren't you piggybacking on someone else's energy?"

"Yes," I reply. "So what?"

My sister Libby is a painter. We take turns playing piggyback.

"I'm calling up to complain," she may say.

"First you, then me," I tell her—and we hold each other's hands across the phone lines.

"But shouldn't you be able to find your discipline within yourself?" spiritual sticklers sometimes badger me.

"Find it where you can, how you can" is my response. I am a working artist. This means I am a pragmatic artist. Support from friends is a sensible workable writing tool, and I use it. Let others pursue the mythological writer-as-heroic-loner position. For myself, I like life a little less lonely, a little more user friendly, a little more all-is-right-with-the-world than writerly. So, yes, I talk to my friends about my writing life the same way someone else might complain about a bad day at the office.

I don't believe in making my writing work into a rarified something that only another writer could understand. My friend Laura teaches gifted children. Since my writer is arguably a gifted child, I find Laura's soothing words a particular balm. Julianna McCarthy, a brilliant and seasoned actress, a brilliant and seasoned friend, faces my rejections and hers with a seasoned sympathy. Rejection is part of the actor's life. It's part of the writer's life as well. A little friendship can go a long way toward salving the wound.

So can a nice dinner out, yet another cheap trick, the Bribe.

"If you write another hour, I'll take you out to dinner," I sometimes bribe my writer. "If you finish the first draft, you can get the navy moiré dress."

Hot fudge sundaes, iced lattes, new frocks, old friends—all these bribes are cheap tricks, and, like racy lingerie in the bedroom, I use them because they work. (New lingerie is another favored bribe for coaxing my writer.) As I've said before, writing and sex strike me as having a great deal in common. In both cases, highbrow and writerly may not get you what you really want. Cheap tricks can.

I have saved the best of cheap tricks until last. That is the Writing

Date. Some of the best dates of my life and some of the best writing that I've done in my life have occurred on Writing Dates.

"Let's go to the coffee bar and write for an hour and a half," I have often said to Mark Bryan when we are living in the same city. We wrote an entire book, *The Money Drunk,* across the table from each other at coffee bars. We both wrote longhand, whispering to each other.

"Let's go to the coffee bar and write for an hour or two," I have often proposed to Tim Wheater when we are traveling and working together. Off we have gone to a coffee bar, restaurant, or even to a quiet living room corner, where we settled in side by side to write on our respective books, mine this one on writing, Wheater's a book on music and sound.

"I need to write. Let's make a date," my friends have been known to urge me, knowing that I am game for an hour or two of shared energy.

"Mom, I'm coming into the city for the weekend, but I need to be able to write. Could we make it a writing weekend?" my daughter, Domenica, phoned me this morning to ask.

There is something enlivening about writing in duos. A great deal of usable track can be laid in chummy proximity. So effective is propinquity at creating courage that Arts Anonymous, the twelve-step program dedicated to creative health, holds a once-weekly writing workshop, where members sit down side by side to attack their blocks on paper.

Cheap tricks are useful. Avoiding cheap tricks, being too pure or too proud for them, can be expensive.

"I'm in the homestretch, pour on some prayers," I have cajoled willing girlfriends, knowing from experience that distant prayers can create very present help and inspiration.

I have had writing friends react with shock when I tell them that I use prayer as a daily tool, a cheap trick, in my work.

"I never pray about my work," they tell me.

"I always pray about my work," I tell them back.

On my side, I would cite centuries of painters and composers who routinely prayed for inspiration. Who am I—and why am I—too modern to avail myself of the same help? For myself, I take the term "Creator" to be quite literal. What I am appealing for—and counting on—is artist-to-artist help. It is my considerable experience, as a teacher and as an artist, that when people ask for creative help, they get it.

A young screenwriter told me: "I got a ride into the city from this girl I didn't know very well. I had just decided I wanted to shoot a five-minute film and needed a good director of photography. She was a director of photography and had just decided she wanted to make a five-minute film for which she needed a writer. We almost drove off the road when we realized we had both gotten exactly what we prayed for."

When I was shooting a feature film, I noticed that my spiritual help often took the form of persistent hunches or intuitions: "This roll of film has a light leak" or "Grab a couple more cutaway shots." Inevitably, when I listened to such guidance, the intuitions paid off. As a pragmatist, I believe in using whatever pays off.

"Was he told when he was young that pain would lead to glory? Will he still believe it when he's dead?" asked the Beatles. Many of us, like the character in the Beatles song, seem to have been raised to feel that in order for something to be "real," it must be difficult. As a pragmatist, I want such thinking to go. There is no reason that work cannot be easy and real. Cheap tricks help to make it that way.

CHEAP TRICKS
Initiation Tool

Set aside one hour. This tool involves some physical as well as psychological ingenuity. You are to build—or rebuild—a writing station. If you have one you already love, you may wish to set up a second one.

A writing station can be as simple as a pot of pens, a pillow to prop your back on, and a well-angled lamp at bedside. A writing station may be as showy as my friend Pam's sky-blue desk with a gold enamel bar marking the spot where she sits to write. For me, the essentials are a cache of pens, a photo of my daughter, a few playful symbols of things I love—a horseshoe for a paperweight, a pinecone to remind me of nature, usually a seven-day candle, a rose Lady of Guadalupe, if possible.

Writing stations should be festive. It helps the play of ideas to have a sense of play. Some writing stations are elaborate and beautiful: a carved teak letter box with curling dragons, a Chinese silk tapestry runner, a tiny vase with a single orchid. Some writing stations are not complete without a source of music. Others are quiet and contemplative, like a writing altar, a stick of incense burning to one side.

In a house shared with others, a writing station might be as minimal as a favorite chair, a good standing lamp, and a flower basket for supplies. What matters is the writing.

STAKES

LIGHTNING BOLTS are dropping to the ridge above my house. The sky is dark. The wind is stiff and the thunder rumbles close and loud. This is dangerous weather, the kind when accidents happen: flash floods, forest fires, sudden death by lightning. I could use this weather in a screenplay. It would raise the stakes.

When people wonder what makes some writing readable and other writing less so, they are centering on the issue of stakes. Stakes are the answer to the question "Why should I care?" The best answer to "Why should I care" is always "Because it matters very very much." As in:

- It is a matter of life and death.
- It will cost or win me a fortune.
- My entire happiness depends on the answer.

In real life, all of us know the issue of stakes: a parent is diagnosed with lung cancer, the sale on the house falls through, your best friend is having an affair, your sister discovers a lump in her breast, your company is being bought out by a large conglomerate that will bring in its own people, putting you out of a job.

In writing, stakes are a question of clarity and empathy. As writers, we must make it very clear what our characters stand to lose or gain so that our readers, encountering these stakes, can feel empathy and care about the outcome.

"Why take the risk?" is the second part of stakes. First, we must know what the risk is. Second, we must know the value system that causes a character to take risks.

I live alone and have lived alone most of my adult life. My animals—horses and dogs—fill my days with companionship. Their happiness matters to me. They contribute highly to my own.

In New Mexico, lightning is far more dangerous than our rattlesnakes. The snakes bite, while the lightning kills. Walking the dogs through the sagebrush is a matter of double vigilance. You must cast an eye toward earth and sky; strikes can come from either direction.

So why walk the dogs through the sagebrush? Because it makes them so happy. And they make me so happy.

The lights just flickered out. Probably the lightning struck one of the big power lines running along the crest of the ridge. Now the lights are back, but the storm is still rumbling and could still be fierce.

In writing the stakes are raised whenever a character—or a character's value system—is threatened. If the ranch has been in the family three generations, losing it is a catastrophe. If you bought it last year and realize you miss the city, losing it is not such a bad thing. In an open marriage, an affair is fair play. In a traditional marriage, an affair is a heartbreak, even a tragedy. Writing that draws us in is writing that tells us the exact nature of the possible loss. It is grounded in specificity:

"My father is buried on our ranch, under the live oak in the pasture with the stream cutting through it. His bones lie just where they're talking about laying the highway . . ."

"Why should I care?" is always the question a reader brings to reading a piece of work. Answering that question and answering it promptly and fully is what we mean when we talk about establishing the stakes. For my money, beautiful writing that ignores the question of stakes is beautiful writing that soon becomes boring.

A heavy rain has started to fall. The smell of wet dust stings the nostrils. Now that the rain is really here, the lightning is retreating. The rains will make the dirt roads slick with mud; falling rocks will plague the canyon. Ten years ago—and this is a true story—a bus driver was making his very last run before retirement through the twisting canyon on a rainy night. The Rio Grande was engorged with rain. The highway beside it was slick and treacherous. A giant boulder teetered loose, plunged to the roadway, and carried the driver's bus straight into the river. The driver was killed.

"On his very last run" makes the story worse, more poignant. It drives home the life-and-death stakes. As a rule of thumb, when I am writing, whether it's a play, a screenplay, an essay, article, or poem, I like to open with the question of stakes.

SURVIVAL

I can imagine a life without you.
A sky with no stars.
A time before language.
A primitive age
With values relating to survival.

I can imagine a world without sound,
In which no bells ring,
In which birds wing silent
Across skies muted by lack of sun.

What I cannot imagine is my survival—
Still living, still breathing,
When it is air that I am missing.

I am trying not to miss you.
I am trying not to breathe.

For the speaker of that poem, love is a matter of life and death. Losing the beloved is very high stakes: "I am trying not to breathe."

For those of us trying to write, learning our own stakes is part of choosing the territory we will write about. I call this finding your "vein of gold." (My book *The Vein of Gold* centers on finding your creative territory and mining it.) For some people, the stakes that interest them are those of love. For others, the stakes that count are family matters, social issues, financial gain or loss. Part of establishing stakes is not only telling the reader what the potential gain or loss is but also how big that looms in the value system of a character. Very often, when a piece of writing fails to satisfy us, it is because the stakes of the story and the character's value system are at odds: the girl wants the boy but gets the great job instead. In art, as in life, such mishaps are frustrating.

Mythologist Joseph Campbell advised those seeking fulfilling lives to follow their bliss. Nowhere is this better advice than in writing. When we choose to write about what we truly care about, when our values and the characters' values coincide, when our stakes and the story's stakes coincide, we write with passion, purity, and purpose. Like those lightning bolts on the ridge, we hit our target and shed some light in the process.

Ever since I was a child, I have hated bullies. In grammar school, one of the boys began beating up on all of the girls. When he beat up my best friend, I marched across the playground and punched him. "Julie hates bullies" has been a determining factor in my writing career. Arguably, my book *The Artist's Way* was written from the same protective impulse as punching out the schoolyard bully. Artist abuse makes me furious . . . so I did something about it.

Mark Bryan was a teenage father who abandoned his toddler son and was haunted for years by the loss. When he grew up, got sober, and surveyed what mattered to him in his life, Bryan sought—and gained—a reconciliation with that son. Writing from a place of passionate commitment, he spent seven years writing and researching *The Prodigal Father,* a book of reconciliation and reunion for "fathers who left children and the children they have left behind."

When a writer writes from the heart of what matters to him personally, the writing is often both personal and powerful. When a writer writes to what he thinks the market needs—writes, in other words, without a personal investment—the standard of writing is often lowered along with the stakes.

Part of our duty as writers is to do the work of honestly determining what matters to us and to try to write about that. This may take a certain amount of courage. This may mean that we do not meet with immediate support from those who make decisions with an eye to the market.

The Artist's Way has now sold upward of a million books. And yet, when I was seeking a publisher for that book, I sent it off to my then agent at the prestigious William Morris Agency.

"Who would want this book?" my agent shot back. "I don't think there's a market for it."

Galvanized by her negativity, I began self-publishing the book. I sold thousands of copies before the work attracted the attention of a new agent, Susan Schulman, a believing agent, who sent it to Tarcher, who became and has remained its publisher. I believe that I wrote it and wrote it well because the stakes of the book were very high and very personal to me. As an artist, I had needed and devised many stratagems for survival, for healing. I believe if the stakes of the book had been lower for me, the book would not be enjoying such a considerable success. If I had accepted the idea that market should determine what I wrote, *The Artist's Way* would not exist.

In casting about for what to write, I have often used a very simple technique. Taking a blank sheet of paper, I list five things that I am currently thinking about. Reading down the list, I pay attention to my inner sense of which topic has the most "charge" for me. That charge is usually an indication that the stakes involved in the topic are high enough for me to write on it well. A list of topics might look like this:

1. Money laundering
2. ESP
3. Child abuse
4. Social injustice, haves and have–nots
5. Aging

Looking over that list, I feel an extra charge on numbers 2 and 3. Looking over my fiction of the past year, I see that I have written extensively on both ESP and child abuse.

As a rule of thumb, I check in with myself and do a "hot" list about every three months. Some topics remain "hot" for years. These are themes I can return to over and over. They are areas where the stakes remain high for me, rooted deeply in my own value system.

When we write from the inside out rather than the outside in, when we write about what most concerns us rather than about what we feel might sell, we often write so well and so persuasively that the market responds to our efforts. It is also true that when we see that the market exists for a topic that is high stakes for us, there is no dishonor in writing to that slice of the market. Then we are in the luxurious position of being able to write both from the inside out and from the outside in. It is only when we try writing from the outside in, writing on a topic that has stakes that are not personally compelling, that we run the risk of writing thinly and unpersuasively. I, for example, have turned down requests that I write a beauty book. I have, on the other hand, written often and well on the dangerous intersection of sex and violence—an area where for me, as a woman and a parent, the stakes run very high.

Shakespeare's fool Polonius gave the very best advice when it comes to writing and stakes: "To thine own self be true. It will then follow as night the day. Thou canst not then be false to any man."

STAKES
Initiation Tool

This is a tool of self-inventory. One more time you are asked to observe yourself as a character and learn from that observation the nature of your own character.

Clear yourself an hour's writing time "out." Settle yourself with a good cappuccino, a cup of tea, a glass of lemonade or soda. Put pen to paper and answer these questions:

   1.   What three topics do you often read about?

      1.

      2.

      3.

2.   What three topics do you often think about?

    1.

    2.

    3.

3.   What are five of your favorite books?

    1.

    2.

    3.

    4.

    5.

4.   What do these books have in common concerning theme, genre, setting, and, above all, stakes? What do people stand to win or lose? Love, money, health, life, death?

5.   What are five of your favorite movies?

    1.

    2.

    3.

    4.

    5.

6.   What do your movies have in common with your books in terms of theme, genre, setting, and, above all, stakes?

7.   What is your favorite fairy tale?

8.   What is your favorite childhood book?

9.   What do your fairy-tale and childhood book have in common?

10.   List five topics you are currently thinking about.

    1.

    2.

    3.

    4.

    5.

Which of these feels "hottest"?

PROCRASTINATION

I'll begin with the punch line: I've been putting off writing this essay. Writers write and writers procrastinate, but they do it in the opposite order.

"I think I'm writing something really good right now," George, a writer, called to tell me. "Maybe that's why I can barely stand to let myself do it."

"By the third sentence in, I'm just fine," claims poet James Nave. "It's getting to the first two sentences that nearly kills me."

A primary reason writers procrastinate is in order to build up a sense of deadline. Deadlines create a flow of adrenaline. Adrenaline medicates and overwhelms the censor. Writers procrastinate so that when they finally get to writing, they can get past the censor.

What writers tell themselves while they procrastinate is that they just don't have enough ideas yet, and when they do, then they'll start writing. It actually works exactly backward. When we start to write, we prime the pump and the flow of ideas begins to move. It is the act of writing that calls ideas forward, not ideas that call forward writing.

Writers procrastinate because they do not feel inspired. Feeling inspired is a luxury. Writing, often excellent writing, can be done without the benefit of feeling inspired.

Writers procrastinate because it keeps them stuck on one project and allows them to fantasize about the rest, about what they will write when they have time. This keeps the risk low. A writer doesn't have to write anything until what he's currently writing is over with so if that can just drag on a little longer, everyone can stay nice and safe.

Writers procrastinate as part of a writing ritual. Most writers do not want to learn how rapidly and easily they could actually write and so they circle the desk a few thousand times like dogs looking for a comfortable spot to lie down. The idea that in order to write they need simply start writing is not welcome news. Writers become addicted to procrastination. It gives them something to do instead of writing: namely, they can hate themselves. A writer who is not writing is generally filled with self-loathing and self-recrimination. Procrastination is a lot like a drinking problem: it's your own guilty little secret.

Writers have many and varied stratagems for procrastination. Many do it by talking on the phone. "I'll just return a few calls so my mind is clear to write," they say. Other writers procrastinate by reading. They can always find one more thing somehow related— even homeopathically related—to their topic so they can read someone else's thoughts instead of turning to their own. Still other writers procrastinate by writing itself. They take copious notes about what they will someday write. The notes take the place of writing itself.

Most writers don't want to hear that there are some very straightforward cures for procrastination. A daily habit of Morning Pages will train the censor to stand aside and make procrastination much more difficult to practice on any and all writing. Artist Dates will create an inner welling up of thoughts and ideas that will become more and more pressing to put on the page. Blasting Through Blocks, a quick listing of fears and resentments about a project, will often swiftly clear the channel to write. Above all else, a week of Media Deprivation in which you do not read, watch TV, see movies, or listen to talk radio will force even the most adroit procrastinator toward the page with a certain eagerness.

Procrastination has some payoffs that are hard to give up. Being a blocked writer elicits sympathy. You can get a lot of negative attention by being officially brilliant and blocked. People are far less threatened than they are by people who are brilliant and highly functional.

Another hidden payoff of procrastination is that it allows us to be antisocial or at the very least socially dysfunctional. "I need to write" is a favored excuse for begging out of coffee, dinner, and movie dates. If you are writing, writing freely and frequently, then you have no excuse for not getting out into the flow of life—for many of us a rather threatening proposition.

"I think I may be shooting myself in the foot," Greg tells me. "I'm really on a roll and I am having a terrible time getting myself to the page. It occurs to me that we're not afraid of our lack of talent, we're afraid of our talent itself."

The payoffs for procrastinating, the patent self-destructiveness of indulging in it, none of these things matter as much as the cure for it. Again, this is another way in which procrastination closely resembles a drinking problem: who cares why you drink too much? Just stop it!

And so, how do you just stop it?

1.   Write daily, even if only Morning Pages.
2.   Use tools like Media Deprivation and Blasting Through Blocks to give you a jump start.
3.   Watch your telephone consumption.
4.   Watch your note production.
5.   Set a clock for one half hour's writing time. Pray for the willingness to write—and then write.

At its root, procrastination is an investment in fantasy. We are waiting for that mysterious and wonderful moment when we are not only going to be able to write, we are going to be able to write perfectly. The minute we become willing to write imperfectly, we become able to write. It is helpful to "bust" ourselves on this addiction to perfectionism. Instead of saying "I'm waiting until it feels right to write," try saying, instead, "Oh, I'm being a perfectionist again." Then let yourself write—imperfectly.

PROCRASTINATION
Initiation Tool

Yes, this is a "cute" tool, but it is one which I—and most writers I know—find to be a great bribe to productivity. This tool requires you to spend one hour and twenty dollars in a good office supply store. Buy yourself a good new "fast" pen. Maybe buy some index cards to list scenes on. Get come nice stock paper. Buy envelopes and some stamps. You are to use this tool to deliberately procrastinate about writing.

INTO THE WATER

NEXT TO DIVING into a new novel, play, or movie of my own, there are very few things as exciting to me as starting off a new batch of writers. I feel a deep happiness, a profound excitement, as the class gathers. I have been teaching now for two decades, and I can still remember specific rooms, the precise way the light fell across certain faces twenty years ago. I remember, too, my feeling of a glowing secret certainty, what I knew that the class didn't: they would write and write well.

I normally teach a twelve-week writing course divided into three one-month segments. I begin all writers, seasoned or new, the same way, with the assignment of three daily longhand pages of morning writing. These Morning Pages are the absolute bedrock of a writing life. Strictly stream of consciousness, they cannot be done "wrong" and so they teach writers to write freely. They train the censor to stand aside and simply let you write. Typically, writers rail against Morning Pages but become quickly addicted to them as well. Morning Pages are step one in turning on the inner lights of a writer.

After Morning Pages are in place for a month, I ask the students to leave the Morning Pages in place and additionally embark on writing what I call a Narrative Time Line. This is a longhand autobiographical account of their own life—an assignment students typically find daunting. The time lines are to be completed within a month. Telling them to take a cue from the old detective Joe Friday, I ask them to write "just the facts, ma'am, just the facts."

Writing "just the facts," feelings inevitably arise, as do insights and deep connections. Above all, what arises is a sense of fascination and self-worth regarding the incidents of one's own life. Inevitably, certain episodes and people beg for deeper writing than the mere facts will allow. These people and incidents form the basis for "cups." Cups are the basis for the third month of writing work.

My term "cup" comes from a gold-mining term "cupel." That is a prospector's tool used to scoop and sort gold from dross. This is precisely what I ask students to do next. Go back through their Narrative Time Lines and "scoop" out cups of time, writing on a specific memory, episode, person, or theme. Cups, normally running several thousand words in length, from three to five typed pages, are dense in detail and sensory recall. They are ideal treatments for later plays, film scripts, short stories, even novels.

"I don't think it's possible to do Morning Pages without being tipped over into writing," says Daniel, who began with Morning Pages and went on to several movies and two novels to date.

"I don't think it's possible to do a Narrative Time Line without sort of falling in love with yourself and your material," says Evelyn, an actress-turned-writer courtesy of her work with the Narrative Time Line.

"I've gotten six projects directly out of cups," I'm told by Theo, a young playwright and independent filmmaker.

My books *The Artist's Way* and *The Vein of Gold* describe these practices at great and encouraging length. The description, however, matters less than the prescription. What I have just described is sufficient information to launch any beginning writer and to "rehab" any stymied writer. The trick is to make this prescription nonnegotiable and to simply do it. This is what Roethke meant, telling us, "We learn by going where we have to go." Where we have to go is home to the page, and the exercises described in this essay are the surefire route for doing it.

INTO THE WATER
Initiation Tool

Call a friend and set a one-hour writing date "out." Go to your date armed with your fastest writing pen and an unused lined notebook, preferably 8½ by 11. Settle in across from your friend, set pen to page, and begin writing your Narrative Time Line.

The Narrative Time Line is best written in five-year intervals and focuses on what—for you—were the major people and events of your life. The intention of the Narrative Time Line is to give you an overview of your life from your own perspective. It means that your emphasis may be quite different from that of your official family version. For example, the family line may go "And then we moved to a wonderful house in the country." Writing your Narrative Time Line, you might discover you hated that move and that house.

The rewards of doing a Narrative Time Line are enormous. It helps you to win free a version of yourself that is self-determined and autonomous. Students often make connections that have eluded them in years of talk therapy. Many students are heartened to discover their own life contains fascinating material. Fears of "not being original enough" are set aside as their own origins are explored and found to be rich and potent writing material. As a writing teacher, Carol Bly, has said, this tool moves students past a rote, "canned" version of themselves and into an authentic voice. Write your Time Line in one-hour segments.

It is my strong suggestion that you use the buddy system to accomplish this tool. Tell your friends what you're up to, make phone calls for support, and schedule writing dates to help you go the distance.

THE RIGHT TO WRITE

L<small>AST NIGHT</small> I <small>HAD</small> a Great Writer over to dinner. He was one of a dozen people, all invited for roast chicken, corn-bread stuffing, salad, biscuits, and homemade pies—strawberry, peach, and cherry. It was a perfect summer evening and a perfect dinner. The conversation went around like the biscuits, everybody taking their turn and everybody sharing . . . until the Great Writer started talking about writing.

"There are too many people writing now," he grumped. "There are too many people who want to call themselves writers. I lived without heat to be a writer. I suffered . . ."

I nodded politely, determined not to get into it. I knew this soliloquy of the Great Writer. I knew the garret and the whole starving-artist story line—complete with the omitted wife so it all sounded like he did it with no support, no cheering section, and no fun at all. I wasn't going to be baited. My dinner guests, all of whom knew I saw writing very differently, kept flashing me glances. Was I going to let him get away with this elitist stuff? (Yes, the stuffing was delicious and he was just a stuffed shirt.)

"What does suffering have to do with art? What does no heat have to do with anything?" my daughter, Domenica, finally piped up. The Great Writer ignored her.

"I've suffered," the writer continued. "I fought to be a writer. That's how it was done in my day, only the strong survived."

A pall fell over the table. A great many of the diners loved to write, but none was so illustrious as the curmudgeon holding forth.

The Great Writer continued. "I don't mind if people write to express themselves, but they shouldn't call themselves writers or really call it writing. They're not real writers. And you, Julia, with that book of yours [*The Artist's Way*], I don't care if four million people buy it. All it's good for is propping up tables. Everybody shouldn't write. All that slush keeps the good writers from being published. Writing isn't for amateurs."

Now he had me.

"I'm offended," I said. "I'm offended for me and for everybody else you're talking about. I believe people have the right to write. I don't believe that writers are like salmon and the truly gifted and strong are the ones who make it. I think—I know from my teaching—that some of the most beautiful voices we have have been silenced. They had a cruel teacher or parent, some creative accident or mishap. If I can help restore those voices—that's what I am after. Some of my students are in their mid-fifties and have always wanted to write, and when they do they write like angels. We all have the right to write."

The Great Writer glowered. "So what do you want me to do? Leave?"

"Stop being such a _____ in my face at my dinner table," I said. "Have some pie."

"No, thank you."

And the Great Writer huffed off to the living room to sulk while the rest of us finished eating. When coffee was served, a young woman painter drifted in to sit by his side. He began holding forth again.

"I tell my students Joyce was a great writer. Joyce I would give an A. All of you in here, the best you can get from me is an A minus unless you can show me you've got something more than Joyce." The Great Writer pontificated.

Trying to concentrate on my slice of strawberry pie, I found my stomach twisting in knots. This Great Writer ran a creative writing program. He should have spelled it "pogrom." I winced at the damage his competitive machismo could do to a sensitive young writer.

As the evening wound down, the Great Writer came up to say good-bye.

"You'll really hate what I am writing now," I told him. "I am arguing that the term 'writer' should be abolished. I am arguing that everybody should write. That we should have a million amateur writers making novels just for the hell of it. Hell, we all begin as amateurs. Have you forgotten that?"

The Great Writer clearly had. He began to backpedal. "We're all worms," he said. "I'd use anybody's book but my own for toilet paper."

With that he left.

After he had gone, the rest of the dinner party sat around and played detox.

"I've heard that line of his forever," Nave said. "It's just elitist posturing. What's worse, it's one step away from censorship. Only 'Great Writers' should be allowed to write? Who decides who they are? Doesn't it come down, then, to approving of what they decide to write? I think it does. And that is censorship. What's he so threatened about? He's got a little club and he wants to keep everybody out."

I want to let everybody in. I want us all to write. I want us to remember that we used to write. Before phones, we wrote each other letters. We're doing it again with e-mail, and I think it's a balancing of the wheel. We have been going too fast and we know that. Taking the time to write something down grounds us. Taking the time to write how we feel helps us to know how we feel. Taking the time to write to each other, we find ourselves doing more right by each other. Yes, I want a revolution.

I want us to take back the power into our own hands. I want us to remember we have choices and voices. I want us to right our world, and writing is the tool I feel helps us to do it. We are a restless lot here in the West. We do not take easily to meditation. Writing is an active form of meditation that lets us examine our lives and see where and how we can alter them to make them more sound.

Yes, writing is an art, but "art" is part of the verb "to be"—as in

"Thou art truly human." To be truly human, we all have the right to make art. We all have the right to write.

THE RIGHT TO WRITE
Initiation Tool

Set aside one hour's time. Light a candle, cue up some stirring music, set a sacred atmosphere. You are asked to make a contract with yourself concerning your writing. Contracts should include:

- A ninety-day commitment to Morning Pages
- A commitment to finish your Narrative Time Line
- A commitment to write five further "cups" drawn from your Time Line
- A commitment to a weekly Artist Date excursion to nurture you writer and fill the well

Write your contract out formally, date it, and sign it. Congratulations.

Suggested Readings

Please consider this list a "sampler" of titles that may entice you.

Aftel, Mandy. *The Story of Your Life—Becoming the Author of Your Experience*. New York: Simon & Schuster, 1996. Persuasive and useful.

Bennett, Hal Zina. *Write from the Heart: Unleashing the Power of Your Creativity*. Novato, Calif.: Nataraj Publishing, 1995. Kind and comforting.

Block, Lawrence. *Telling Lies for Fun and Profit*. New York: William Morrow, 1991. Good shirtsleeves advice.

Bly, Carol. *The Passionate Accurate Story*. Minneapolis: Milkweed Editions, 1990. Passionate, accurate.

Bradburg, Ray. *Zen and the Art of Writing*. New York: Bantam, 1990. Opinionated, peppery, vital.

Brande, Dorothea. *Becoming a Writer*. 1934. Reprint. Los Angeles: Jeremy P. Tarcher, 1981. The best book on writing I've ever found.

Burnham, Sophy. *For Writers Only*. New York: Ballantine Books, 1994. Prickly and provocative "field report" on writers and writing.

Capacchione, Lucia M. A. *The Power of Your Other Hand*. North Hollywood, Calif.: Newcastle Publishing Co., Inc. 1988. Provocative and playful.

Collier, Oscar, with Frances Spatz Leighton. *How to Write and Sell Your First Novel*. Cincinnati, Ohio: Writers Digest Book. Friendly, practical, grounded, and inspirational.

Elbow, Peter. *Writing Without Teachers*. New York: Oxford University Press, 1973. Radical and catalytic.

Goldberg, Bonni. *Room to Write: Daily Invitations to a Writer's Life.* New York: Jeremy P. Tarcher/Putnam, 1996. A masterfully provocative and wise writer's tool.

Goldberg, Natalie. *Writing Down the Bones—Freeing the Writer Within.* Boston: Shambhala Publications, Inc., 1986. Simply the best into-the-water book ever written.

———. *Wild Mind—Living the Writer's Life.* New York: Bantam Books. 1990. Zesty as New Mexico chile.

———. *Living Color.* Bantam, 1997. A mixed media treat.

Kaufman, Millard. *Plots and Characters: A Screenwriter on Screenwriting.* Los Angeles: Really Great Books, 1999. Straight talk from the horse's mouth. The legendary screenwriter and author of *Bad Day at Black Rock* and *Raintree County* opens his tool kit on screenwriting and the screenwriter's life.

Lamott, Anne. *Bird by Bird.* New York: Bantam Doubleday Dell, 1994. Finely wrought and writerly.

Metzger, Deena. *Writing for Your Life: A Guide and Companion to the Inner Worlds.* San Francisco: HarperSanFrancisco, 1992. Writing as healing.

Nelson, Victoria. *On Written Block.* New York: Houghton Mifflin, 1993. Block as building block.

O'Connor, Patricia T. *Woe Is I.* New York: Grosset/Putnam, 1996. A witty and pointed guide.

Rainer, Tristine. *Your Life as Story.* Jeremy P. Tarcher/Putnam, 1997. Autobiography as art.

Rico, Gabriele Lusser. *Writing the Natural Way.* Los Angeles: Jeremy P. Tarcher, Inc., 1983.

Selling, Bernard. *Writing from Within: A Unique Guide to Writing Your Life Stories.* Alameda, Calif.: Hunter House, 1988. User friendly.

Shaughnessy, Susan. *Walking on Alligators.* San Francisco: HarperSanFrancisco, 1993. Excellent daily companion in a writer's life.

Smith, Michael C., and Suzanne Greenberg. *Everyday Creative Writing.* Lincolnwood, Ill.: NTC Publishing, 1996. Creative, challenging, homey, and fun.

Strunk, Jr., William, and E. B. White. *The Elements of Style.* Needham, Mass.: Allyn Bacon, 1979. Grammatical Bauhaus. The classic.

Ueland, Brenda. *If You Want to Write.* 2nd ed. 1938. Reprint. St. Paul, Minn.: Schubert, 1983. Lucid and seminal.

About the Author

Julia Cameron is the author of seventeen books, fiction and nonfiction, many plays and movies. She happily lives again in the high desert of New Mexico where she busies herself with musicals, movies, poetry, horses, and dogs. No longer a public teacher, she taught extensively for two decades in venues ranging from London to Los Angeles, from Esalen to the *New York Times*. Her work on creativity features the bestselling books *The Artist's Way, The Vein of Gold,* and *The Right to Write*.